Training
For The
Small
Business

Training
For The
Small
Business

How To Make The Most
Of All The Opportunities

Jenny Barnett and Liz Graham

**KOGAN
PAGE**

First published in 1992

Kogan Page Limited
120 Pentonville Road
London N1 9JN

© Jenny Barnett & Liz Graham, 1992

British Library Cataloguing in Publication Data

A CIP record for this book is available from the British Library.

ISBN 0 7494 0725 5

Typeset by Witwell Ltd, Southport

Printed and bound in Great Britain by
Biddles Ltd, Guildford and King's Lynn

Contents

5

Foreword

This book is for small businesses which want to develop to meet the challenges of the future.

You must read it – there aren't many books like it around. It will help you make things happen, not just read and think about them!

We hope that by reading this book your business will begin to make the most of opportunities for learning both inside and outside the business, and so maximise its most important resource – its people.

Section I Looking Inside Your Business

CHAPTER 1

Making the Most of Your Business

Introduction

In this first chapter, with the focus primarily on doing business in changing times, we cover three things:

The background to business – the context in which you operate and the reasons why responsiveness and adaptability are so crucial to success and to survival!

The book and its structure – how it has been designed and written to help you tackle the key factors in making the most of the people in your business.

The business – enabling you to take stock of where you are now in order to find your starting point and then to use the ideas in the book to build on what you have already.

The background to business

As the world changes, so does business. Businesses large and small have both to respond to changes, and also to initiate changes if they want to stay ahead of the game.

Think about the changes which we have seen happening all around us in recent times; huge in their numbers and in the scope of their implications:

- the opening up of world markets with the collapse of the Eastern bloc;

- the development of the single European market;
- the development of more service industries and decline of some manufacturing industries;
- more customer-awareness even among large bureaucracies;
- the increasing focus on letting the market place lead;
- changes in population patterns so that there are now far fewer young people entering the labour force;
- changes in working patterns as the era of the long-service watch disappears and people start to move between jobs and even take time off working to be with families or to study;
- an increasing use of and reliance upon new technology in every sphere of life;
- a developing awareness of environmental issues.

It is not too long before the influences of the changes are filtered down into local factors to which your business is forced to respond (see Figure 1.1).

Responding to these changes is only half the story. Consciously to seek out new opportunities is the other half. What have seemed to be pressures bearing down on the business can be transformed into opportunities to be exploited, and give you new ideas for spotting future trends and patterns which could develop your business even further (see Figure 1.2).

Finding ways to reverse the arrows, as shown in Figures 1.1 and 1.2, will be the key to your business success. Focusing on just one of the external pressures highlighted gives us an example of this. Changing working patterns and the effects of technology upon our lives offer opportunities to alter staffing structures within your business. Many businesses could benefit from staff working from home, equipped with a terminal and fax machine. Staff would still have clear objectives and targets to meet, but could operate more flexibly than previously. Businesses would still achieve their goals, but could save significantly on the overhead costs of expensive office space.

To cope with this everyone in the business needs to be involved. The heads-down, 'this is the way we have always done things round here' approach is not going to be enough for the businesses of the 1990s – it is new skills which will be needed:

- thinking creatively;
- using imagination to see possibilities;

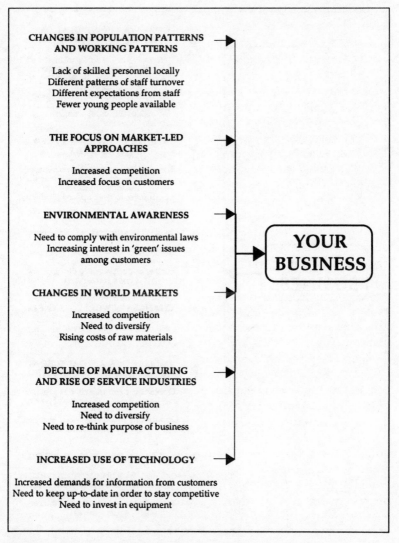

CHANGES IN POPULATION PATTERNS
AND WORKING PATTERNS

Lack of skilled personnel locally
Different patterns of staff turnover
Different expectations from staff
Fewer young people available

THE FOCUS ON MARKET-LED
APPROACHES

Increased competition
Increased focus on customers

ENVIRONMENTAL AWARENESS

Need to comply with environmental laws
Increasing interest in 'green' issues
among customers

CHANGES IN WORLD MARKETS

Increased competition
Need to diversify
Rising costs of raw materials

DECLINE OF MANUFACTURING
AND RISE OF SERVICE INDUSTRIES

Increased competition
Need to diversify
Need to re-think purpose of business

INCREASED USE OF TECHNOLOGY

Increased demands for information from customers
Need to keep up-to-date in order to stay competitive
Need to invest in equipment

YOUR
BUSINESS

Figure 1.1 *External changes: pressures and effects on businesses*

- possessing the vision to see what might be.

These skills are going to mean the difference between survival and decline.

The approach of businesses may have enabled them to be

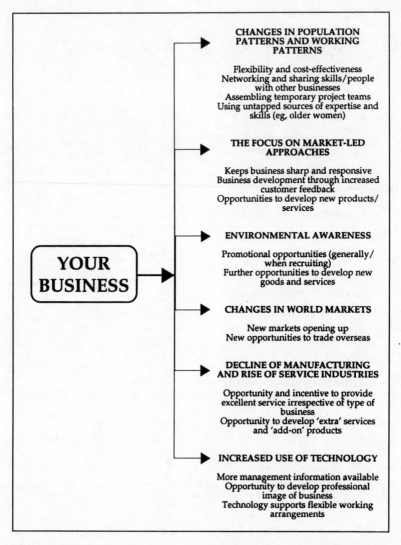

Figure 1.2 *Reversing the pattern: turning pressures into opportunities*

efficient in former, more stable times. However, in the current constantly changing climate, new approaches are necessary to enable business to be both efficient and effective (see Figure 1.3).

All of this adds up to one thing: making the most of what you have got in your business and developing your people so that they

Efficient businesses	Effective businesses
are bound by constraints	look for opportunities
dwell on, and in, the past	discover new ways for the future
value a 'quiet life'	value argument
encourage belief in existing systems	encourage doubt
focus on quality control and inspection	focus on customer requirements through quality philosophy
want to control their people	want their people to control themselves
eliminate mistakes	learn from mistakes

Figure 1.3 *The difference between efficiency and effectiveness*

want to **learn** continually. It is then that your business will have begun to make the most of its own resources by **taking stock** of what it has, **finding out** about new ideas and initiatives and **building on these and moving on**. This book will tackle systematically these three activities as applied to training and developing your people.

This book

Why this book?

It has been written:

- to help **you** make the most of the people in your business;

– to help **them** to make the most of the many opportunities for learning and being trained, both inside and outside the business.

Many books have been written about starting up a business. Indeed you may wander down the high street and pick up leaflets, information packs in banks, libraries, job centres and careers offices, etc. Over the past decade or so, the government and other organisations have put much money into the 'start-up' process with a range of awards, grants, trusts and support services.

Much too has been written about 'Organisational Development' and 'Human Resource Development' – valuable and interesting, but, as the terms imply, rather theoretical and not always relevant to the smaller business! Yet, again and again we read in newspapers and listen to politicians speaking of the importance of training in the continued success of businesses.

Recognising that smaller businesses are often very squeezed and pressed for time and resources, this book has been written to give, in a straightforward and practical form, a range of ideas and approaches for training people cost-effectively: **achieving maximum learning for minimum cost**.

For whom has it been written?

We hope this book could prove useful to **anyone** in **any organisation**! In particular it is aimed at those in small and medium sized companies, probably with less than 100 people, who do not have a training/personnel 'specialist'. We believe the contents are relevant and applicable to a very wide range of organisations:

- manufacturing companies;
- shops;
- service sector – leisure and tourism, cleaning, health and care, etc.;
- commerce – insurance companies, building societies, etc.;
- professional practices – doctors, architects, accountants, solicitors, etc.;
- schools and colleges;
- voluntary organisations – church, parish councils, school governors and many other community groups;
- units, divisions, departments, etc. of large organisations, particularly where these are encouraged to be self-managing and independent.

Many people in these organisations are aware of the value of training, can readily recognise improvements which need making in their organisations but are unsure perhaps about how to set about it. The 'training industry' itself has become quite widespread with a great range of businesses offering training and associated services and many books, materials, videos, television programmes, etc. contributing to its promotion. It can all be rather confusing to an interested non-specialist. We hope to unravel some of the tangle!

What is in the book?
The book is divided into two sections.

Section I: Looking Inside Your Business concentrates on people and activities largely within your business. We have begun with this as we believe, as a result of our experiences working with businesses, that until these components and activities are in place, you will not make the most of training. It is too easy to start with the outer ring – to buy in training or advice from the outside – and then find that most of the value disappears, rather like matter into a black hole! The training is not applied, the learning is lost and the business fails to make tangible gains or improvements. The training is thus seen as a waste of time and money. So, we recommend a start by 'looking in' at your business and concentrating some time and energy getting certain things in place, before rushing out to buy in anything!

Section II: Looking Outside Your Business concentrates on the range of organisations and services around to support and supplement your training. It will enable you to make informed decisions about who or what to use, and how to make the most of what you do decide to buy in. It is important at times to consider training opportunities outside your business, even if you are successfully making the most of things inside. There is a danger of becoming too inward-looking and out of touch; fresh ideas and approaches can be invaluable in ensuring your business stays sharp and competitive.

When you are making the most of opportunities for training and encouraging learning **inside** your business, then you are likely to make the most of those **outside**. The different components are shown jig-saw fashion: they lock together to add up to the whole picture of effective training (see Figure 1.6).

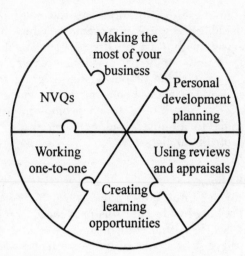

Figure 1.4 *Looking inside your business: the necessary components for effective learning and training*

Each chapter of the book is sub-divided into three parts:

1 Taking stock
2 Finding out
3 Building and moving on

1 Taking stock
This part invites you to look at how things are in your business at the moment to make sure you recognise what you already have, what currently works well and can be further developed. It is so easy to 'throw the baby out with the bathwater' when new ideas are presented. It makes sense to combine the best of the old with the best of the new! Carrying out a stocktake before exploring and/or introducing new ideas does avoid, too, the sudden threat of sweeping change. People are generally much happier to try out new things if they themselves have identified what does need changing or improving. Involving them in the taking stock process should help this and minimise resistance!

2 Finding out
This second part should give you some new ideas! It contains information, guidelines, checklists and suggestions for you to

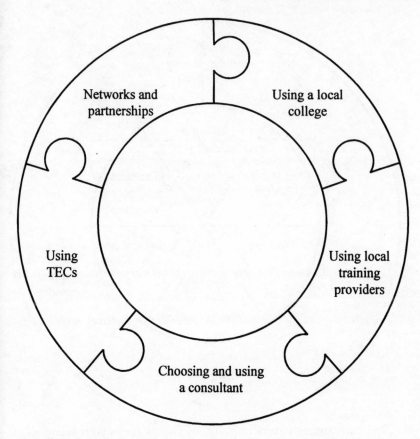

Figure 1.5 *Looking outside your business: making the most of external opportunities and resources*

consider and discuss. Some things you may already know well and be using and others may be quite new to you. Clearly, you would be unwise to try implementing all suggestions immediately – this section can be referred to again and again over a period of time with different members of staff.

3 Building and moving on
This final part of each chapter brings together both the previous parts. It looks at how to use and apply the findings from part two and build on what you already have as identified in part one. There are suggestions for action planning – how to introduce and

19

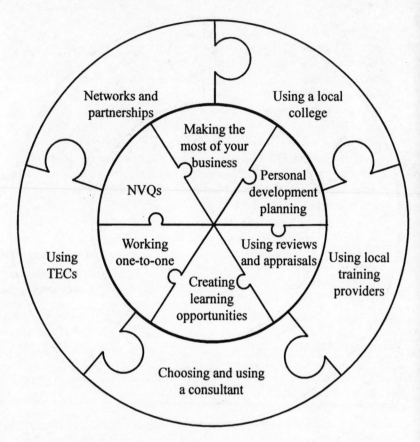

Figure 1.6 *Looking at the complete picture: making the most of opportunities inside and outside the business*

implement new ideas and changes in a suitable way for your business. It is obviously very important that you adapt and modify our ideas to take account of your business, the people who work within it and the way you like to tackle things.

How should you use this book?

Read through to get an overview – we hope this should be easy to do as we have tried to keep the jargon out and the ideas practical!

Jot down any key points or things which you feel are particularly important, considering the suggested activities – what you might wish to tackle first and how.

Pass the book around – or buy more copies and encourage others to read and consider the ideas!

Focus your energies on Section I initially – looking inside your business and getting things right here is so important.

Consider who else in your business should be involved and how to involve them. There are numerous opportunities for involving others – each chapter begins with a taking stock activity. It would be easy to share these out and see each one as a project for one or two people to tackle. The more people who are involved the less work falls on one person and the more commitment to new ideas you are likely to gain.

Use your thoughts, notes and those of other people to discuss and agree an overall plan for tackling training over the next year. Try to be realistic; it is better to identify and agree one or two priorities, set some clear objectives and achieve some measurable results, rather than be over-ambitious and lose heart!

Your business

In this chapter so far we have considered the background to your business – the changes and developments likely to affect you – and outlined the thinking behind the book and its structure. Before tackling any of the suggestions in the following chapters, we feel it is essential first to take stock of your own business: your plans, your people, your problems. This will encourage introducing new ideas gradually in a planned and unthreatening way.

A business stocktake

A simple way of taking stock of your business to gain an overall picture is to carry out a SWOT analysis – to look at:

Strengths
Weaknesses
Opportunities
Threats

Use the format in Figure 1.7 to think of as many opportunities and

Looking inside the business at:

STRENGTHS   WEAKNESSES

Looking outside the business at:

OPPORTUNITIES   THREATS

Figure 1.7 *The SWOT analysis*

threats as you can which your business currently faces from outside (eg, increased competition, different potential markets, lack of skilled job applicants, recession, etc.) The first section in this chapter on **Background** should help.

Then focus on the strengths and weaknesses your business has in the face of these (eg, hard-working, committed managers, up-to-date equipment, resistance to new ideas, problems with secretarial support, etc.). Put in as much detail as you can. It is well worth asking other people with whom you work to do this either with you, or separately: different opinions can be very revealing!

Key issues and training requirements will often depend on factors such as the size, age and type of your business. Use the chart in Figure 1.8 to prompt thought and discussion about your current situation.

Your business situation	Likely plans and problems	Likely demands on people
A new business – small, recently formed	Getting established, surviving the start-up difficulties Cash flow Getting and keeping customers Making decisions about how to operate Finding and obtaining resources and equipment Costing and pricing	Energy, determination and enthusiasm Flexibility – being able and willing to tackle a wide range of tasks Using initiative and persistence – making contacts and finding customers Learning quickly – from mistakes and from other people
A growing business – still quite small but rapidly developing	How to manage growth – should we increase customers or extend range of products/services or both How to keep control over what is happening Possible need to invest in new premises and equipment – cash flow	Recruiting and training new staff – how many and what skills do they need? How to use and incorporate new staff with new ideas and build effective teams How to decide on roles and responsibilities, more staff, fewer tasks, more specialisation
A mature business – been established for a while but still expanding	May well have developed more complex systems to control activity Set procedures and policies to ensure all people treated fairly and consistently Danger of becoming too paper-bound Slower to change and respond to customer needs and market opportunities Communication not as quick and effective Expansion geographically and in range of products/ services – how far to take it How to keep competitive	People have increasingly specialist roles – how to keep communciation effective and ensure individuals and teams work together well for the benefit of the whole business How to keep common sense of purpose How to keep energy, initiative and new ideas coming and prevent people getting too hide-bound and resistant to change More opportunities for training within the business and more need for developing specialist skills

Your business situation	Likely plans and problems	Likely demands on people
An older business – stable or in decline	A lot of 'red tape'	People work to their job descriptions and may be unwilling to look for new and better ways of doing things
	Possibly out of touch withcustomers and their needs – danger of newer, smaller businesses taking customers away	
	Set ways of doing things	Good people leave if there is no room for them to grow and develop
	May well have built up strong community links and be well known and trusted	New people are expected to fit in rather than bring in new ideas and approaches
	Need to re-energise, re-form to make smaller, more responsive units or shed some of current work and re-define purpose and goals	New initiatives in training and development needed – to encourage people to apply experience and skills to new products, services and approaches
		Need to find ways of encouraging and rewarding change, improvements, ideas and suggestions from everyone

Figure 1.8 *Your business situation, plans, problems and demands*

Your business situation in the 'life cycle'

Having looked through the chart, you will probably have recognised various things which apply to your business. Like people, businesses are all unique, however, and it is unlikely your business will fit neatly into any one category! You will probably need to reflect on and answer the questions listed below.

What is your business situation?
What are your plans and priorities?
What are the main problems facing you?
What are the key people issues?

Healthy businesses

You might also like to consider the following checklist and see how your business compares.

Checklist of Characteristics of Healthy Organisations
Healthy organisations:

- are clear about their objectives and tasks and the roles and responsibilities of their people
- give systematic feedback to people about performance as an accepted routine activity
- offer scope for people to influence the setting of objectives, targets and the judgement of their performance
- pay careful attention to people's needs for recognition, achievement and job satisfaction
- make sure individuals feel valued and that their needs are important enough to warrant attention
- recognise and reward good performance
- carry out appraisals which focus on development and NOT on judgement
- have a real commitment to developing people and show this by the behaviour and standards of all the senior people

---

Having carried out the SWOT, the life cycle analysis and considered the healthy organisation characteristics, consider the following questions:

Where does our business need to concentrate its efforts?
What do we want to see more of in our business?
What do we want to see less of?
What do we want to stay the same?

You should now be able to set some specific goals and clear, measureable targets for your business. You might wish to separate these into short and longer term items, eg:

In a year's time we will have achieved the following . . .
In three years' time we will have . . .

Goals, targets and training needs
As part of this taking stock process of your business, it is worth thinking about the skills people need to have and to develop, particularly in the light of the key issues and goals you have been

identifying. The checklist is offered as a starting point, but you will need to adapt and add to the list to cover the necessary aspects of your business.

You may find it helpful to use the following key:

We have considerable experience and skill in this area, put these into practice and ensure new ideas and skills are developed.

We have some experience and skill in this area but we recognise we need to develop these and require further training.

We have little or no skill or experience in this area and feel it is a priority for the business.

We have little or no skill or experience in this area but do not consider it to be a priority at the present time.

Checklist for Analysing your Current Level of Skills		
Aspects of the Business	Current Skills	Details/ Comment
General aspects – applying to all businesses		
Business planning Setting out aims and detailing how they will be achieved	☐	
Marketing Researching the market, and identifying potential customers and their needs	☐	
Devising a marketing plan	☐	
Promoting, advertising, etc. goods and services	☐	

Customer care – gaining, keeping
and making most of customers ☐

Exporting ☐

Accounting and finance
Book-keeping and accounting
techniques ☐

Understanding and using financial
information ☐

Dealing with personal and business
taxation ☐

Using computers to support
systems and provide information ☐

Managing people
Recruiting and selecting people ☐

Making the most of people –
training, appraising and developing ☐

Effective communications: ☐

   face to face ☐

   by telephone ☐

   in writing ☐

Negotiating and dealing with
difficult situations ☐

**General management and personal
skills**
Planning, problem-solving and
decision-making ☐

Managing time, stress and crises ☐

Employment law; health and safety,
equal opportunities legislation,
import/export regulations ☐

Quality management and quality
standards (eg, BS5750) ☐

Computers and other technology ☐

**Other specialist aspects relating to
your business**

☐

This should have given you a general profile of your business situation and the overall training needs and priorities. It will provide the foundation for all the other chapters in the book, particularly the 'Taking Stock' activities.

CHAPTER 2
Personal Development Planning

Introduction

This chapter looks at a central issue in the area of developing people, that of personal development planning, and focuses on involving everyone. This means making sure that each person employed in your business has a clear plan outlining his or her training and development needs over a certain period of time. Without such plans people cannot make the most of opportunities for learning new skills, gaining new knowledge and developing new areas of expertise. If opportunities are planned and structured properly, with time built in for people to review what they have learned and to make sense of it in their day-to-day work context, then those people have a better chance of making good progress.

Taking stock

How do you plan training?

How effectively does your business develop the people within it? Below is a series of short exercises and questions to help you establish whether personal development planning is currently an issue within your business, and whether its introduction would benefit the business, now and for the future.

You, as the owner/manager probably have a clear idea of where the areas to be developed are in your business, what the goals are for the next few years and where the potential lies for growth. Is the same true of the rest of your team?

Interview as many people as you can in your business about

any training or development in which they have been involved over the past, say, five years.

Ask yourself and the staff:

How were they selected for training?
What was the training they received?
Did it help them do their job better?
Did it help them develop new skills for the future?
Who followed up the training with them? (Talked it through, made sure that they were given the chance to put into practice the skills which had been learned?)

Ask yourself:

Does the training and development currently being provided actually meet the needs of:
– the individuals with whom you spoke?
– the business – not only now but for the future?
Do staff actually know what is expected of them?

Find out whether staff:

know where the business is going
know what are the targets to be met
know how these may affect what they are doing and what training they might need to cope with new targets
have really thought about their jobs, and whether training or support could help them to carry out tasks more effectively
have really thought about any extra things they could learn which would enrich their job, or develop new aspects of the job

Ask other people's advice about this issue. Talk to your business associates about how they plan and structure training and development for their staff.

Is there a pattern to their responses?
Is there one way which seems particularly effective?
Are they doing more or less than you are in this area?

The answers to the above questions should give you some idea of whether enough planning of individual development is taking place, or whether it is in fact a bit 'ad-hoc', as and when it is needed. We can look at this in more detail in the next section.

Finding out

What is personal development planning?

Often, what passes for personal development planning in reality lacks the final 'p' – planning. You may have been feeling quite good as you started to read this chapter, knowing that staff are regularly attending training events of one sort or another. Indeed training courses are often seen as the answer to staff training needs. However, sending people away on courses may sound effective at the time you make the booking, but all too often courses:

- are unrelated to the needs of the organisation and the individual;
- do not make effective links between theory and practice;
- are not reviewed or evaluated properly and are a substitute for real development.

Real development should enable individuals to grow and be ready to meet the changes and challenges they will certainly face, and the organisation to become a place where learning is allowed and respected and which continually re-evaluates the way in which it operates.

The best way to explain the importance of personal development planning is by looking at the training cycle (see Figure 2.1). When considering training and development for an individual all aspects of the cycle need to be in place before that training can be really effective.

Personal development planning is the process during which the first two parts of the training cycle take place. After that the training can be delivered, or opportunities made available for the individual to learn, in a variety of different ways. Chapter 5, Creating Learning Opportunities, examines this part of the cycle in more detail. Reviewing what has happened and how effective it

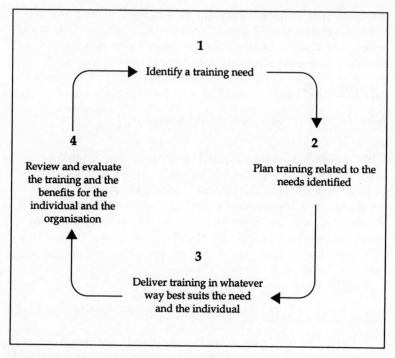

1

Identify a training need

4

Review and evaluate
the training and the
benefits for the
individual and the
organisation

2

Plan training related to the
needs identified

3

Deliver training in whatever
way best suits the need
and the individual

Figure 2.1 *The training cycle*

has been is explored further in Chapter 4, Using Reviews and
Appraisals.

You can probably see this if you look again at the answers which
you received to the questions posed in the Taking Stock section
above. You may have found that all too often training has been
seen as something quite separate from the needs of the business,
and often the business has been a real block to an individual's
development. Sometimes people return from training courses
fired up, only to find that the organisation is not ready yet for the
changes that they would like to implement as a result of some new
idea or skill gained from the training. It is of no benefit to your
staff or the business if some form of training and development has
taken place without proper planning (the 'identification of needs'
part of the cycle above) or follow-up (the 'review' part of the cycle
above). Only proper planning will ensure that the person understands why the training is needed, and only proper follow-up will
ensure that real use is made of that training.

What affects the personal development plan?

1 Business objectives

In the first chapter of this book we looked at the need for every business to examine its business targets and to set itself clear goals. Staff may need your support to help them to help the business meet these goals. This is where a clear plan for each individual which outlines the support which staff feel they need and the ways in which this support will be given will be most beneficial.

For example, you may have set yourself a business goal of:

finding 50 new customers for our X product

which will be achieved by:

- writing new promotional literature;
- attending more trade shows;
- contacting all past customers of Y product to inform them of the X product.

The skills and knowledge involved in just this one goal you have identified are:

- writing skills – editing, proof reading, designing layouts;
- technical knowledge of X product;
- ability to communicate clearly with customers;
- tele-sales skills;
- organisational skills to compile database of past customers and then compile results of survey.

It may be that these skills and knowledge are:

- new for your organisation;
- not new, but those people who already possess similar skills could do with extra support to enable them to achieve even higher standards.

Either way, planning for people to be able to cope will help to ensure that the goal is met in full.

2 Changes in an individual's role

New business objectives can sometimes mean that an individual has to develop in different areas. Sometimes changes in role occur because of the need for an individual member of staff to change direction: for personal satisfaction, career progression, to allow someone else to take over some responsibilities. Individual members of staff may find therefore that new skills and knowledge are called for. This too needs to be taken into consideration when planning that individual's development needs.

3 Developments outside current responsibilities

Sometimes an individual can elect to undertake some training or development outside company time for personal satisfaction. The far-seeing manager may choose to look at this carefully before dismissing it as a personal hobby or interest which has no bearing upon an individual's job. The unlikeliest pursuits if reviewed properly with you can hold all sorts of hidden spin-offs for the business. The very fact that someone is learning can be used positively as a way of enticing that person to view job-related learning with the same enthusiasm, and some outside interests can yield achievements which are easily transferred to the business.

For example, one of your staff may be studying public speaking in her spare time, another may be taking art and design classes, another cordon bleu cookery! With a little imagination some of these talents can be harnessed for the business. The skills and confidence gained by public speaking, art and design and cookery could, for example, be useful for promotional events which in the past you have paid other people to organise.

So, consider carefully what you choose to see as 'job-related training'. You may not wish to fund all of your staff's spare time activities, but support in some form could reap benefits for you and them in the long run.

What is involved in putting together a personal development plan?

Figure 2.2 shows the elements which combine to make the personal development plan.

The plan itself can be completed in a series of phases, as follows:

Phase 1: Looking at the business objectives
Phase 2: Defining roles and responsibilities within the business

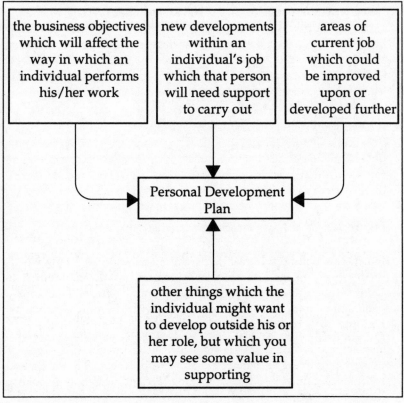

Figure 2.2 *The elements which contribute to the personal development plan*

Phase 3: Identifying development needs
Phase 4: Identifying how needs will be met
Phase 5: Reviewing the personal development plan

We will look at these one at a time. Use the example of a personal development plan shown in Figure 2.3 to help you.

Phase 1: Looking at the business objectives
Look at the business targets with each of your staff. Examine them to see whether there are any implications for them. For example, one of your objectives might be to improve the quality of your communications with customers, and one of the ways in

Business objectives	My respon- sibilities	Development areas: skills/ knowledge	Approach to learning	Review date

Figure 2.3 *Example of a personal development plan*

which this will be achieved is by the installation of a new word-processing package and new laser printer. At the moment it is your receptionist who types all letters and who will obviously need some support in getting to grips with the new equipment. List any such objectives which affect a person's role in the first column of the personal development plan shown in Figure 2.3.

Phase 2: Defining roles and responsibilities within your business
In other words, give some thought to who does what. This will entail identifying who is currently responsible for performing certain tasks and roles, and whether new business objectives will take individuals into hitherto uncharted waters! You can enter these details in the second column of the personal development plan.

You will need to examine each person's role in terms of the skills and knowledge required (see Chapter 6, National Vocational Qualifications, for more on this). This will help you plan exactly what the training and development needs are for each person in very specific terms. For instance, the receptionist in the example above needs to develop the manual skills of using the new keyboard layout and of loading the paper tray into the laser printer, but also the knowledge of what to do in the event of something not working properly, which way the paper goes into the printer, how much time each print job takes and so on.

Identifying skills and knowledge required in the performance of a job will make the whole process more effective.

Phase 3: Identifying development needs
New business objectives may mean new demands of staff. New demands mean new skills and individuals need to be able to talk these through with you. Of course there will also be plenty of times where nothing new is demanded of a person but where there is scope to perform even better, and this needs addressing also. This is a sensitive phase in the personal development planning process. Individuals may feel that their competence is being unfairly doubted and may need re-assurance that development is a necessary and important part of everybody's existence to ensure that the business goes from strength to strength. Make sure that you recognise the strengths of the individual before talking about development needs. Often people will be only too delighted that new opportunities for growth are being presented, and will seize those opportunities readily. Enter what you agree on the personal development plan in the third column.

Phase 4: Identifying how needs will be met
For people to develop they do not have to attend courses. Development can mean reading trade journals regularly, reading about some new ideas in the person's field of work which will give new insight, observing a colleague carrying out tasks, discussing different ways of doing things with colleagues (see Chapter 5, Creating Learning Opportunities, for more on this theme).

Remember: think creatively and cost-effectively.

Be sure to think carefully about matching the most appropriate type of development to the needs of the individual. For example, it might be considered a good idea for the receptionist in the example above to read through the accompanying manuals. This would of course explain which key controls which function, how to make back-up discs, how to merge documents, etc. However, some people, and the receptionist may be among them, do not learn best from reading, but learn most effectively by a hands-on approach, and would pause to refer to the manual only when a particular function needed explanation.

It is worth bearing in mind, therefore, before completing this part of the personal development plan that there are usually two

---

Activity-based, Practical Learners

• like to get involved immediately and enthusiastically
• are open minded and will try anything once
• like the excitement of a new challenge
• like to try things out for themselves to see if they work in practice
• prefer to get on with things and act quickly once they know they work

Thoughtful, Logical Learners

• like to stand back and think about things before rushing in
• like to watch and listen before joining in
• collect lots of information about events before coming to any conclusion
• like to think things through in a step-by-step way, fitting things that they are learning into a rational pattern

---

Figure 2.4 *Different approaches to learning*

main ways that people like to learn. Often a pattern can be seen in individuals, so that one 'style' becomes the preferred one.

For example, if you were told that you needed to learn a foreign language because an exciting and potentially lucrative business opportunity was on the horizon in another country, how would you go about doing it? One person might rush over to the country and immerse him or herself completely in the language and the way of life. Another might start reading grammar and phrase books.

In terms of learning, people tend to fall into being activity-based and practical learners, or thoughtful and logical learners (see Figure 2.4).

The success, or not, of an individual's personal development plan will be influenced by the way in which that individual elected to learn, so spend some time talking this through with each person before deciding on the best action to take.

For example, a member of staff's role has expanded to include tele-sales. A training need has been identified for the person's development plan, and you are deciding between you the best way to meet this need. You could:

- send the person on a course to learn about tele-sales;
- ask the person to work-shadow a colleague who is experienced in this field;
- put the person into the sales department with a case-load to pursue, to try out selling in this way.

Which one you decide upon should take into account the person's preferred learning style. Someone who is an activity-based, practical learner may relish the opportunity to become immediately involved in a department. Someone who is more of a thoughtful, logical learner may feel ill at ease with this approach, and welcome the idea of work-shadowing a colleague before having to cope with the job for real.

Whatever it is that you decide between you to do, it should be entered on the personal development plan in the fourth column.

Phase 5: Reviewing the personal development plan
Like everything, not much benefit will come from the developments you have agreed upon if they are not reviewed carefully. Has the development helped? What benefits has the individual gained? How has the organisation gained? It will be important to review what is happening continually with individuals, and it is also useful to set yourself and the person clear targets for review so that you can ensure that the proposed development will take place. The personal development plan review can form a part of the appraisal interview, for it is at this time that whole work roles can be looked at (see Chapter 4, Using Reviews and Appraisals, for more on this).

Building and moving on

Personal development planning is crucial to the successful and on-going development of the business as a whole. You will need to consider the following, however, so that you and your staff gain the most from it:

- How will I introduce personal development planning to staff?
- Who will be responsible for coordinating the activity?
- When will I start the whole process?

• How should I tie in personal development planning with the setting of business objectives?

Below is a checklist of benefits which could help you introduce the activity with your team.

Benefits of Personal Development Planning

• It is supported from the top and shows you are interested in staff development and are prepared to put time in to demonstrate that commitment
• Staff are being valued for what they are doing – they are being given the opportunity to talk about what they are achieving and given the opportunity to take things further
• It is a morale boost – it shows everyone that your business knows where it is going and has the professional systems to back this up
• It can form the basis of structured career development for everyone – and it is supported by you
• It develops the team to work more effectively – to be more dynamic, responsive and forward looking
• It moves the whole organisation forward.

How many more can you think of?

Getting started
A structured approach to planning development for individuals will help to keep the whole thing very simple.

• Arrange some time to have a discussion with each member of staff.
• Be sure to let everyone know exactly why you want the meeting (make sure that all staff know that everyone is looking at this issue. If individuals start thinking that they have been 'singled out' they might feel threatened by the idea of a meeting).
• Ask staff to give some thought to what support they feel they need to do their job better. Rather than doing all this within

your meeting, ask people to come prepared by considering the exercise below.
• Ask them to bring it with them to your meeting and it can inform your discussion about their role. This sort of exercise can highlight all sorts of inconsistencies and overlaps in what people think they should be doing, and actually do in practice – be prepared!

Putting into action
Once the idea of personal development planning has taken root in your business you should be well on the way to ensuring that

---

EXERCISE TO HELP ME CONSIDER MY ROLE

Your job can be seen as a blend of:

Demands: things you must do, about which you have no real choice – the core of your role (the inner circle in the diagram below – see Figure 2.6)

Constraints: the boundary or limit of your role (the outer circle below) – the extent to which your role goes.

Choices: things which may not be strictly part of your job description, but which you choose to do because you enjoy them.

Have a go at completing the doughnut diagram to represent what you do in the following way:

1. List all the tasks that you carry out.
2. Decide whether they are choices or demands and write into the appropriate space of the doughnut.
3. Underline anything which you feel you could do better with more knowledge or enhanced skills.
4. Think about how you would like to see your role shaping up in the future. Have a go at drawing the doughnut again and include on it any new areas which you would like to have a go at within your role.

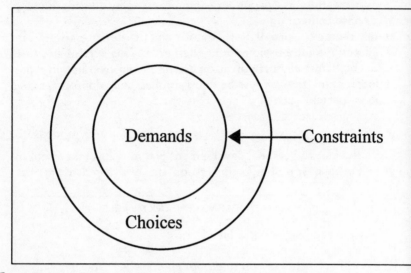

Figure 2.6 *Your job/role: demands, constraints and choices*

constant progression for individuals and, therefore, for the business as a whole, is seen as the norm.

Make sure that you keep the ball rolling. In Chapter 4, Using Reviews and Appraisals, you will find more detail on the subject of continual review. This will be vital if people are going to feel that their progress matters and continues to matter – that it was not just a 'flavour of the month' initiative. You will need to think about:

- who should have the responsibility for the personal development planning of each member of staff – if your organisation is small it may be that you yourself carry this out with staff; if it is medium sized there may already be somebody in charge of staff development who would be the obvious choice;
- how to involve staff in and inform them of the business objectives (see above) for the coming period of time, as these will affect their training and development needs.

Consider how you will:

- review progress – and who will be responsible;

- evaluate the success of the ways in which you and the individual decided to learn new skills or acquire new knowledge;
- make time for people to reflect on what they are learning;
- allow time for people to get together and share what they are doing – this way everyone learns from everyone else;
- build your appraisal system to incorporate a look at the personal development plans – see Chapter 4, Using Reviews and Appraisals, for more on this
- build up your own personal development plan – who identifies your own training and development needs?

CHAPTER 3
Working One-to-One

Introduction

This chapter focuses on how a range of one-to-one situations can be used as learning and training opportunities, and on personal responsibility. We learn from other individuals in many ways: watching and listening, modelling ourselves on them, using their actions and approaches, asking their advice and opinions before making our own decisions. We learn, too, from their mistakes: rejecting their approaches and even doing the opposite if we feel their actions are inappropriate or counter-productive!

Often this learning is informal and unrecognised. It can, however, be one of the **most effective** and **least costly** ways of training, or providing structured opportunities for learning. A system of mentoring can work very well. In one organisation we know, mentoring is carried right the way to the top. Even the chief executive has a mentor (his second-in-command) who regularly discusses the performance and style of his boss with the aim of improving both.

Taking stock

Who are your experts?

Everyone has strengths. Doubtless you can readily identify individuals in your organisation who have special skills and to whom others go for advice and help.

Is there someone, possibly a youngster, who is a whizz at sorting out problems with computers?
Is there anyone, possibly an older person, who is skilled at

Individual	Expertise/support used by others

Figure 3.1 *Current sources of expert help*

defusing potentially explosive situations and calming down angry customers?
Is there a lively, confident extrovert who has great success in making new contacts or giving presentations?
Is there a good organiser who manages to keep a number of projects and activities all ticking over at once?
Is there a good writer who can communicate clearly, simply and effectively on paper?

Effective organisations have effective people using their talents to the full: the right people in the right jobs. Use the following questions to prompt a stocktake of the 'mentors' in your business – those to whom others turn when they have a problem.

Where do I/others in go for help and advice in our company?
What kind of help do we look for: professional, legal, technical, specialist, general problem solving, difficult situations, personal concerns?

You may find it helps to draw up a table (see Figure 3.1).

How, if at all, is this expertise and support recognised? Informally, by word of mouth? Formally through job description, time allocation, reward, status?
Are there ways in which we systematically plan and use the skills of others in a training and learning one-to-one situation?

For example:

- training and supporting young people as employees, trainees or on work experience;
- training newcomers to the organisation;
- training and supporting people when they take on new roles and responsibilities;
- getting to grips with new equipment, systems and procedures;
- when people leave or have to be made redundant;
- for developing managers and supervisors.

Looking at your notes and observations as prompted by the questions and other discussions you may have had, consider how well the current situation is working. Some tactful exploration and discussion will probably be required if you are to gain a complete and accurate picture!

How willing are people to use and be used by each other to train and learn?
Can you identify situations where this seems to work particularly well in a one-to-one situation for both parties?
What about problems? Can you think of instances where things did not work out at all well?
What were the reasons for the good and less successful attempts?

Having investigated how people use each other to learn, it is worth carrying out a stocktake of the skills, experience and qualifications people have acquired in teaching, training, instructing, supporting. Many people have developed these outside paid employment:

- as parents;
- through involvement in community groups: scouts, guides, youth clubs, playgroups, churches, etc.;
- with sports and leisure activities: coaching and training others; through other voluntary activities: marriage guidance, advice
- bureaux, school governors, primary/nursery classroom assistants;

- through evening classes: studying for teaching qualifications, or running leisure and adult education sessions.

Are you aware of the hidden skills people may have?

It is possible that within your organisation you may have a wealth of experience and expertise in individuals used to helping others learn. However, they themselves may be reluctant to acknowledge or own these skills or be lacking in the confidence to use them fully. So how can you find out? It will largely depend on the size of your organisation, the systems and procedures you have in place and the 'way we do things around here'. It might be through:

- individual informal discussion;
- through a formal review/appraisal system if there is one;
- by questionnaire (with careful explanation!);
- through staff meetings;
- as a research project for someone as part of his/her own development.

Having worked through this section and carried out the suggested activities, you should now have a clearer, up-to-date picture of how the one-to-one situation is used in your organisation, who uses whom and for what and the skills and experiences already around.

It is worth standing back from your own organisation and considering some ideas about how you might further develop and improve what you already have.

Finding out

The traditional approach

'Sitting by Nellie' has been the traditional and rather *ad hoc* way of teaching an individual new skills. The learner picked up skills and knowledge by watching, listening to and copying a more experienced worker. Along with the skills, however, many faults and poor procedures could be picked up and the whole situation could be ineffective if the experienced worker was not very good at or interested in training someone else. So the 'Nellie' system has had its critics and many larger organisations opted for the systematic training method, using a training specialist, taking the training away from the 'shop floor'. There tends to be a pattern of throwing out much of the value of an old system when something apparently better comes along. The 'Nellie' system had its faults but it had its strengths too, particularly when both parties were enthusiastic and committed:

• individual attention, support and encouragement;
• an appropriate pace for learning;
• learning in the real situation with all the problems that involves;
• the opportunity to ask questions when necessary, as problems arise;
• the approach can be geared to the individual's current skill level and preferred way of learning;
• there is the opportunity to check out and give feedback immediately.

The right approach and system for you

Ideally, the training and learning one-to-one system will build on the best of what has happened in the past, but look to make it more effective and organised. The main differences between the former 'Nellie' system and the suggestions following are that the latter are:

• carefully planned;
• involve preparation and training of the experienced person;
• developed within a framework of clear objectives and regular reviews.

Depending on your type and size of organisation, the business, people and training needs, there are a number of things you might consider.

– a mentoring system where experienced and knowledgeable people are identified to guide and support others who are new

to the organisation or who are taking up new roles and increased responsibilities;
- a coaching system where skilled and experienced people are used to train others in using new equipment, carrying out new tasks, systems and approaches;
- a counselling system where one or two carefully chosen and trained people are there to help others deal with problems, stress, difficult situations, worries etc. of a more general nature;
- a co-counselling/learner partner system where individuals with similar roles/responsibilities, status, projects, etc. work together to help and support each other.

It is worth exploring these terms further; Figure 3.2 gives an indication of the different emphasis.

There is much overlap: the skills which contribute to successful coaching are likely to lead to someone who is effective in a counselling situation, but this may not always be true. An experienced worker may be very effective at coaching: training another person in a particular skill, good at asking questions, picking up anxieties, making things clear and simple but lack the patience and empathy required in counselling which is much more of a passive, non-directive role. An effective counsellor may be unwilling or unable to give the clear guidelines, direction and intervention which a mentor may need to do if she or he is to prevent a newcomer making a costly and potentially disastrous mistake!

You will need to consider carefully what **you** want from a one-to-one system in your organisation and design it to meet your needs and make the most of the people you have. When you come to negotiating changes and developments in people's roles and responsibilities, you will need to be very clear what you are asking them to do. The various checklists which follow in this section should help.

Responsibilities of the trainer in the one-to-one situation
The trainer's role might tend be that of mentor, coach, counsellor, learning partner or any combination. You will need to define both the role and the responsibilities. You might include some of the following:

• to guide and support individuals new to the organisation and

Mentor	Coach	Counsellor
Supports others	Guides others' actions	Helps others to identify problems, issues and possible solutions for themselves
Shares experience	Tells and shows: acts as an instructor by	
Has sound knowledge and understanding of the company and its business	– breaking down task – demonstrating – correcting others	
		Does not advise or make specific suggestions – uses a non-directive approach
Has credibility	Focuses on achieving competence in a particular task	
Encourages others to see opportunities for development and helps them through the learning process	Tends to be a one-way learning process with a clear superior-subordinate relationship	Encourages reflection and talking around issues
		Allows others to lead and determine the direction
Has a sound understanding of the different ways in which people learn	Is good at explaining and clarifying, offering suggestions for making task easier	Uses open questions to help others explore ideas, feelings and thoughts
Challenges and helps others to learn from their experience and action	Is skilled at the task in hand	
		More of a passive role, listens very actively and carefully, speaks to clarify and probe
Questions where necessary, points out problems and suggests alternatives.		
Focus on LEARNING: supporting the learner through the learning process, widening terms of reference to maximise learning	**Focus on the TASK:** breaking a learning task into manageable bits and ensuring learner competence in each	**Focus on a PERSON:** enabling an individual to explore situations and responses

Figure 3.2 *Roles in supporting the one-to-one situation*

help them settle in smoothly and become effective as soon as possible;
• to support, encourage and help individuals grappling with increased responsibilities, new equipment or procedures;

- to challenge and question where someone appears to be mishandling a situation and where necessary intervene to prevent costly error;
- to instruct, explain and inform where individuals need to develop new skills and knowledge to tackle a particular task;
- to review and give constructive criticism on an individual's performance to enable him or her to learn from daily experience and activity;
- to listen and probe with careful questioning to help individuals explore problems and work through the decision-making process;
- to help and support individuals when they may be struggling or stressed and, where necessary, suggest and encourage new approaches and changes.

However, this is not to suggest that in a one-to-one training session the trainer has to adapt one role to the exclusion of the others. There needs to be an appropriate response to the problem, the learner and the situation. The trainer may focus on one particular approach by adopting one of the roles yet have the other two ready to draw on as necessary.

An example of one-to-one training in action
A learner may seek and want strong direction, particularly if not feeling confident about tackling a new task. She or he may want to be told clearly how to do something. However, meeting this immediate request may not necessarily be the only or most appropriate response. In the following dialogue you might like to consider the responses made by M (the mentor) to L (the learner).

First approach
L   I've got to go to DG Electrics tomorrow to deal with a rather sticky complaint. You know the Managing Director there don't you? Bad tempered, very critical but a good customer. How would you tackle it?

M   Well, it depends . . . What's the problem?

L   Thompson, the MD, he's the problem – miserable old so and so. I know exactly what will happen when I walk in. He'll look me up and down, ask where Jane is in a condescending way and then launch into a full scale tirade against us – me in particular.

51

M   You sound as though you are expecting a repeat of a previous experience. . . .

L   Well, yes and no. I've not had to go before but I've heard Jane talk about it when she comes back from DG Electrics and she's always in a foul mood for the rest of the day. No-one dares to stand up to Thompson because he gives us such good orders.

H   It seems as though there is a history of problems. What do you know about past dealings and difficulties with the company and how they have come about?

L   Not much . . . only that since we introduced the new computer system there have been some delivery problems and invoice errors.

M   Mmmmm . . .

L   But I don't know all the ins and outs. I suppose he's a bit twitchy with all the mistakes on the past few orders.

M   That's good – you've got a picture of his situation. Can you think of any more information that might be useful prior to your meeting?

L   Well, I suppose I ought to pin down exactly what's been happening with his company . . . list the errors with dates and try to find the causes and what we've done or planned to do to improve things. But that's not going to help me cope with his ranting and raving. I shall probably lose my temper or panic or be rendered totally dumb!

M   Why do you think Jane has asked you to go – remembering the importance of DG as a customer?

L   She **said** she thought I was ready to deal with a difficult customer and that a fresh face might be a useful way of reviving a rather rocky relationship!

M   I think she's right. You handled the flak at the Tuesday meeting very calmly. You listened carefully, made your points firmly and rather than trying to score points remained positive and looked for practical solutions. All of that will stand you in good stead with Mr. Thompson! Now, shall we consider some of his likely complaints and how you might respond. . . .

Second approach

L   I've got to go to DG Electrics tomorrow to deal with a rather sticky complaint. You know the Managing Director

there don't you? Bad tempered, very critical but a good
customer. How would you tackle it?

M   Well there are six things I always remember when dealing
with complaints:
– collect all the information
– check out the facts with everyone concerned
– identify the problem
– agree the course of action with the customer
– make sure the agreed action is taken
– write and circulate a brief report when appropriate.

L   Oh, right, I'll just jot those down. Can you repeat them
please?

There are obvious advantages and disadvantages with each of the
responses outlined above, as there would be with other possible
approaches. The approach will have to take into account things
such as time available, the urgency and importance of the situation as well as the individual person and problem.
     You might like to consider the following questions after reading
through and thinking about the example above.

Which response is most immediately helpful?
Which response best prepares the learner for the meeting?
Which response supports the learning process most
effectively?
Which requires most skill on the part of the mentor?
How would you have reacted to each question from the
learner?
How would you feel after the two versions of the mentor
response?

One-to-one training: skills checklists
Effective use of the one-to-one situation for training and learning
obviously requires careful thought and sensitive handling. In
addition, it requires considerable skill from **both** parties if the
most is to be gained. The key skills which both will need to
develop are all related to effective **communication**:

• listening
• questioning

53

- giving and receiving feedback (constructive comment and criticism of performance)
- being assertive
- explaining things clearly and logically.

It is not easy to communicate well: individuals are complex and unique and one can never be sure of their reactions! However, encouraging people to use the following guidelines and practise the skills should gradually help everyone make the most of one-to-one learning opportunities.

Checklist 1: Guidelines for Effective Listening

- Be patient: it is too easy to challenge or dismiss before fully understanding.
- Judge and assess the content only: it is too easy to be put off if someone is rambling or hesitant.
- Keep an open mind: avoid over-reacting to loaded words.
- Listen for ideas and themes: it is too easy to nit-pick on facts and details and put someone off.
- Ask for examples and further information, showing you are following and interested.
- Use encouraging non-verbal communication: head nods, smiles, occasional words.
- Allow silence: it is too easy to jump in before someone has finished trying to explain a difficult situation; use a quiet question, or reflect back the last comment if the other person is obviously floundering.
- Repeat back and summarise at appropriate intervals to make sure you have really heard and understood what the person is saying or implying.
- Don't fall into the trap of thinking about what to say in reply and forming advice and judgements which may be inappropriate.
- Avoid letting other things distract: telephone, visitors, etc.

Checklist 2: Guidelines for Effective Questioning

- Be careful and aware of the tone of your voice: it is too easy for questioning to become interrogation!
- Use open questions to encourage someone to talk or expand: questions which don't invite a simple yes/no, for example:
    'What have you found most challenging in your new job?'
    'How did yesterday's meeting go?'
- Use a comparative question if the person is struggling, for example:
    'How does this system compare with the one you used in your last job?'
    'What did you feel was different about today's meeting compared with the one last week?'
- Watch for the reactions to certain questions and back off or re-phrase if the person is obviously uncomfortable; this will only block any useful learning.
- In any session where you are using questioning it is worth starting with simple, factual, specific questions and moving gradually on to more searching ones such as those which deal with feelings, reactions, opinions, problems.
- Avoid using the following:
    leading questions, where there is an expected response – 'Wouldn't it be stupid to waste money by . . .?'
    judgemental questions – 'Why on earth did you do that?'
    multiple questions, where the other person doesn't get a chance to answer – 'Who chaired the meeting and what was the main point of discussion and did anyone object to the timescale for introducing the new computers, and, by the way which sort have they decided to buy?'

Checklist 3: Guidelines for Giving Effective Explanations and Information

Prepare carefully by thinking about:

- What you want to put across: how much detail, depth.
- The person with whom you are dealing:
    current level of understanding, knowledge or experience
    personality
    what you know about how she or he likes to approach and
        learn things.
- How you might wish to put things across:
    in small manageable chunks
    giving an overview to start with
    posing questions
    giving examples or demonstrations
    using diagrams
    key points written up.
- The resources, equipment, time and room you have available.
- The sequencing and timing of the various points you wish to make.
- How and when to get the other person involved; when to use questions to check understanding; when to invite questions and discussion.
- What you might produce for the other to take away to work on: checklists, reminder sheet, key words, rhymes, mnemonics, etc.

Checklist 4: Guidelines for Giving and Receiving Feedback Effectively

Giving feedback:

- Start with the positive, but don't build up to a big 'BUT'! Look for ways of building on achievements:
    I've noticed how calmly you handle difficult customers **and now** you need to make sure that the agreed action is always carried out immediately.
- Be specific: vague and generalised comments do not make it easy to accept or act.

- Focus on things which can be changed. There is no point in telling someone they need to be taller to give an effective presentation. You could usefully suggest that careful positioning of self and equipment will ensure that people will be able to see the presenter.
- Offer constructive criticism with carefully thought out alternatives and suggestions.
- Be prepared to take personal responsibility for the feedback you give and avoid making generalisations, for example:
  'I noticed my concentration lapsing when you . . .'
  rather than:
  'You were boring when . . .'.

Receiving feedback:
- Listen; don't reject or argue. It's very difficult to give honest feedback and all too easy for the receiver to become defensive.
- Make sure you really understand what is being said; it's too easy to over-react to certain words and miss the context or meaning of what is being said.
- Ask for feedback when you want it and ask for it to be specific, eg, 'I have to make my first presentation to the senior managers this afternoon; I would be grateful if you would discuss the content and my delivery of this afterwards, particularly if I presented the statistics clearly'.
- Use the feedback to reflect, learn and develop. It might be worth jotting down key points when receiving constructive criticism and taking time to think around what you did and what was said and planning how to change things for the better next time.
- Thank the giver even though receiving the feedback may not have been easy: few people like criticism even when well intentioned. However, it is difficult to give and can be a very effective way of learning from your own experience.

Checklist 5: Guidelines for Communicating Assertively

- Know what you want to say and be brief, clear, to the point.
- Use 'I' statements ('I think') indicating that you recognise they are your thoughts and state opinions as opinions not facts.
- Come out with it: be honest and direct rather than hinting or beating round the bush, hoping others will pick up your meaning.
- Give reasons if appropriate but not long-winded explanations, excuses or apologies.
- Be open in sharing your opinions, views and information without putting yourself or other people down.
- Look for ways to get round problems constructively rather than seeking to apportion blame or complain.
- Look people in the eye and try to be relaxed when talking.
- Avoid laughing, moaning or being sarcastic.

If all these checklists and guidelines seem rather overwhelming, remember when you look at them carefully they are really just about encouraging people to work well together: something which is of great concern to **all** organisations at all times! They could be used by all individuals in setting personal plans for improving skills as well as by those involved in supporting the learning of others.

There are some real benefits for individuals in taking on responsibility for training others: developing their skills and career prospects, the satisfaction of seeing others progress, contributing to the effectiveness of the business, status as well as the opportunity to look afresh and critically at their own ways of doing things – possibly coming up with new and better approaches.

For the organisation, training one-to-one 'on the job' is a very cost-effective way of getting relevant training where and when it is most needed: almost impossible to get from outside training providers! In addition, gradually the business will develop its own home-grown trainers so it is always ready to tackle new challenges speedily and effectively. There is nothing like successfully tackling new tasks and responsibilities for motivating and gaining increased commitment from people as well as building a team which works effectively.

Building and moving on

You have been prompted to:

- carry out a stocktake of what is currently happening in training and learning in the one-to-one situation in your organisation;
- consider some ideas and guidelines of how you might develop things further and build on what you already have.

You now need to make some plans and decisions. It is too easy to rush in with new ideas and meet resistance!

Plans and decisions

Try working through the following questions, which could also be the focus of a small group discussion at some point. Refer to Chapter 1 to put your ideas in the context of your business objectives and plans.

> Thinking about our business objectives and training needs for individuals and groups how could some kind of mentoring system be useful to our organisation?
> Who could/would use it?
> What kind of system would best meet our immediate needs? And longer term needs?
> How should we identify appropriate people and how many?
> How should we introduce the idea?
> How should we train identified people, building on what they already have?
> What might be the incentives/pay-backs for people being committed to such a system?
> What might be some of the problems? How can we anticipate and minimise these?

You will find it helpful to refer to other chapters in the book.

- you might wish to introduce the 'mentor' idea through **review**

and appraisal (Chapter 4) when discussing possible new responsibilities with individuals
- you might want everyone to consider how and when access to a mentor might be most helpful as part of **personal development planning** (Chapter 2)
- you might wish to consider how the mentor role could include training and assessment responsibilities to enable members of your staff to obtain **national vocational qualifications** (Chapter 6)
- you might wish to buy in outside training for developing in-house mentors, trainers, etc., and will need to look at **colleges** and other **training providers** (Chapters 7 and 8)
- you might wish to contact your local **Training and Enterprise Council** with a view to getting support, advice and/or funding to help you set up your system (Chapter 10).

Use your thinking and notes to encourage discussion with other people in order to come to a decision about a one-to-one training system: what you would like it to be to give most benefit to your organisation.

You will then need to make some specific plans, relating to a specific training need or problem and identify and brief the people concerned.

Planning in action: an example
A business has two new members of staff: a part-time receptionist and a young trainee, a recent school-leaver.

A mentor system would be an effective way of working them smoothly into the company, giving on-going support. The first few weeks in a new job are always stressful and if they go badly, commitment and motivation are seriously damaged. Some decisions will have to made about possible mentors:

Should there be one person to support both new members of staff?
Or would it be useful to have two mentors who could compare notes and ideas and support each other?
Will the role of the mentor be the same for each newcomer?
If not what are the implications in terms of time, skills, etc.?
Should the mentor(s) be the line manager or supervisor of each,

or from elsewhere in the business? What would be the advantages and disadvantages of each?

How will the idea be introduced to all the people involved and how will they be encouraged to make the most of the opportunity?

How and when will the effectiveness of the mentoring system be reviewed?

You might wish to draft a plan of how you would tackle this situation in your business.

Practicalities

Having firmed up some ideas about the kind of system you want, how it might work and what its objectives are in the first instance, there are more plans to be made about the day-to-day practicalities. Many good ideas founder when the daily pressure of work eats into time allocated for training. You might wish your one-to-one system to be informal with minimal paperwork. The last thing you will be wanting is to impose unnecessary extra work or red-tape! However, to make the most of the one-to-one situation it is worth working through the following questions and perhaps using them as a basis for discussion and planning in your organisation. They could usefully be used by prospective mentor and learner at the start of any planned activity so that each has a clear, agreed way of working.

Planning Checklist
Session diary

- How formally do we want/need to plan sessions?
- How often should we meet?
- Should we diary firm dates for several weeks/months in advance or should we set a particular time each week, for example?
- Where should we meet?
- For how long; should there be a time limit?
- What about incidents/crises/problems which affect planned activity?
- Whose responsibility to organise or re-arrange meetings?

Session agenda

- How and when should we decide the content of sessions?
- Are there items which should **always** be on the agenda?
- Are there items which should **never** be on the agenda (eg, general moans and groans about the organisation)?
- What should be recorded from the sessions and how?
- Do we need a formal review of sessions and if so, when and how should this take place?

Prickly problems

- How could the mentor role potentially conflict with other roles and responsibilities?
- How could this be avoided?
- How do we deal with clashes/differences of opinion?
- What should be our ground rules for running and managing our sessions together?
- What are the issues around openness, honesty and confidentiality?

You should now be at the stage to put your ideas and plans into practice. It is worth starting with a pilot scheme: you certainly wouldn't go into full scale production of a new product without a careful trial period. If things go well you can build on them confidently; if there are problems you can sort them out and try alternatives without jeopardising the whole idea!

CHAPTER 4
Using Reviews and Appraisals

Introduction

Not the wielding of the big stick!

It is a sad fact that the words 'review' and 'appraisal' often result in fear, scepticism, mockery or apathy. Sometimes the negatives are understandable: it is so easy to mismanage the process of looking at people's performance and achievements. Too often it is done without appropriate preparation, as a token gesture, in a heavy-handed way and used for the purpose of redundancy, pay awards (or no pay award!) or for giving someone a good talking to!

Yet it **can** be such an effective way of supporting learning, improving performance and encouraging training and development. In fact used well it can contribute greatly to the success of the business, as people will be encouraged to gain more expertise and give more to their roles. The focus here is on looking back and learning.

Taking stock

So how are things in your organisation? This first section invites you to review and appraise your own review and appraisal processes – both formal and informal. It might be painful, but make it honest!

How do you review past experiences?
Everybody reviews: even a mull over things after a meeting, driving home in the car constitutes a review. Unfortunately, we do not always **learn** as much as we could from the process,

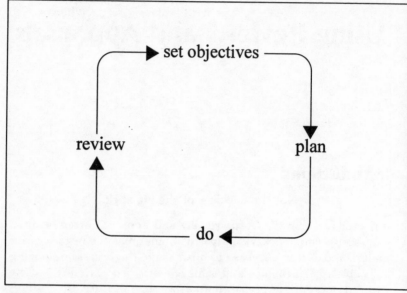

Figure 4.1 *The cycle of effective work*

particularly if the review is carried out alone and nothing is jotted down. Thoughts are forgotten, or seen to lead nowhere or are pushed aside with the pressure of the next day. Reviewing is of course part of the cycle of effective work, as shown in Figure 4.1.

This book has been written in such a way that it encourages a review – a taking stock process – at the beginning of each chapter; if not carried out you are in danger of discarding or failing to make the most of what you already have. So review your own reviewing:

What conscious reviewing takes place in your organisation already? You may find completing – and adding to – the table in Figure 4.2 a useful starting point.

You may wish to add other aspects to this chart and consult with others in completing it. Consider then the following questions:

Are there any gaps?
Anything particularly significant in when and how things are carried out?

What is reviewed	How/with whom	When
The whole business: direction/objectives		
Performance/ achievement of individual people		
Performance/ achievement of groups/teams		
Recruitment/ selection		
Training		
Individual products/ services		
Customers		
Marketing		
Equipment and premises		
Systems and procedures		

Figure 4.2 *An analysis of current review activity*

How do people give and react to constructive comment?

Focusing on people, it is worth thinking about the feedback situation in your organisation. Feedback is a crucial way of involving another person in the review process (see Chapter 3, Working One-to-one, for more detail about good feedback). Use the following questions as a prompt:

65

Do people give and receive constructive criticism openly, honestly and in a positive way?
If not, why do you think this is?
Are there individuals who are particularly good/bad at giving and receiving constructive comment?

Think too, about the way things are done when there are new activities or projects to tackle, or when staff are asked to take on new or different responsibilities:

Is there a conscious process of reviewing previous experience before tackling new things?
What, if any, systems exist to record individual people's or group activity and achievement for use as the basis for review discussions?

How do you judge the performance of your staff?
Reflect also on the formal staff/performance appraisal. You may have found that although you regularly discuss experiences among yourselves in order to improve, a more planned and recorded appraisal system is another matter.

Is there a formal system to look back over a period of time at achievements, problems; to set new targets and explore possible changes in roles and responsibilities?
If there is, how effectively does it work? How do you measure its effectiveness?
How do you know and check out what people feel about it?
How does the appraisal system relate to the business plans and objectives?
If you have no formal system, or have tried one unsuccessfully in the past, what are the reasons or problems?

It is also necessary to consider carefully how people think and feel about the processes of review and appraisal. It may be that in a small business there has been no time to consider the activities mentioned in the questions above, or that they have not been a priority. However, it is unusual to find someone who does not want to know how well s/he is doing, if it is done in an

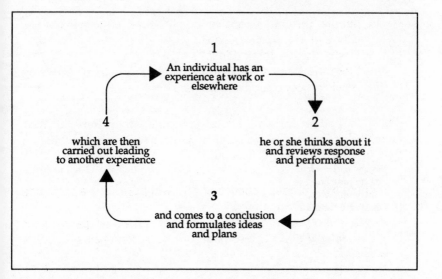

Figure 4.3 *The wheel of learning*

encouraging, positive way. So a stocktake of former experiences is probably useful:

> What experiences (good and bad) have you and others had of performance review and appraisal in the past, elsewhere, going back, perhaps even to school-days?
> Why were these experiences good? Or bad?

You might wish to put out a few feelers to find out how people might respond to reviewing and appraising performance in a more systematic way – to find out fears and concerns and identify what they would and would not like to see in place. This is probably best done through unthreatening, informal discussion.

Finding out

The review process in learning and training

Review is an essential part of learning. The learning process itself can be seen as a wheel as in Figure 4.3. Rather in the same way that spokes keep a wheel taut and effective, the four points on the learning wheel ensure the learning is really effective.

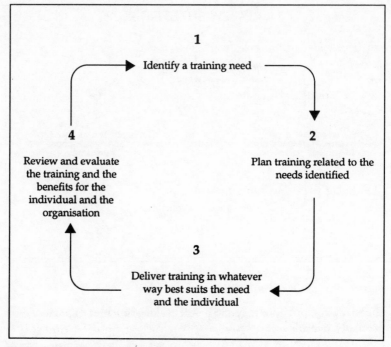

Figure 4.4 *The cycle of training*

The second stage is where review is found. Without careful reflection, looking back over an experience it is less likely an individual will come to the right conclusions and formulate appropriate ideas in order to learn from and build on his or her experience.

When considering the process of training someone, review is again a crucial factor. Training, like many other business activities, works best when all four stages of the cycle in Figure 4.4 are completed.

Having carried out any training it is crucial to look back at what was done and how, what worked and what did not and why. Otherwise, bad practices and unsuccessful approaches will be repeated, wasting time, effort and money!

Self-review and reviewing with others

Without continually reviewing what we do and **learning** from this, we would never make the most of the opportunities around

---

REVIEW SHEET/LOG

What happened – incident or situation:

My reactions/performance:

Results – what worked/what did not:

Learning points to remember in future:

Figure 4.5 *Example of a review log*

and improve our performance. For any individual to review his/ her own work and learn from this may be painful at times. It is sometimes said that 'experience is a hard task-master, for it punishes first and gives the lesson afterwards!'

Discussing experiences one-to-one with another person, particularly a skilled and supportive listener, can be a useful way of reviewing and learning from experience (see Chapter 3, Working One-to-one).

Review 'logs'
As well as talking things through, some people find writing down thoughts, observations and concerns after an experience can be very useful, particularly when trying to come to terms with difficult situations, people or upheavals. A very simple learning log, diary, or review sheet can help to focus thoughts and be used as a reminder before tackling a similar situation again. The example given in Figure 4.5 has been found to work well.

Keeping such a log can be particularly useful for:

• individuals new to a job, or taking on new responsibilities;
• a group or team to use when working on a specific project;

- providing critical incidents to form the basis of discussion with a mentor, supervisor or manager and during a formal appraisal;
- prompting and encouraging people to share experiences and give and receive constructive criticism.

Reviewing in practice

You may have some concerns about the practicalities:

When should reviews take place?
Who should carry them out?
Where should they be done?
How?
What should be reviewed?

It is difficult to answer these questions, as supportive, regular review should be part of normal working practice. It would seem reasonable to suggest that reviewing should happen whenever there is a need. For example:

- a supervisor may wish to review daily the progress, performance and any problems of a youngster on work experience from school or on a youth training programme;
- a new employee may ask his or her line manager, or an experienced person doing a similar job, to review the first month's achievements;
- a project manager may ask a member of the team to review with him the progress and problems to date;
- the manager of a business may be asked by his or her bank to call in for an annual financial review and the manager might well ask another manager within the business, or running another, to review this financial review: how it went, what better preparations need to be made next time, etc.

Thus a review might be prompted by one person wishing to review the performance of another or by someone asking for a review of his or her own performance. To make the most of the process, it is wise to be quite specific:

'I would like to meet you on Friday morning at 10.30 for half an hour to review your first week in accounts. In particular I would like to talk about the computer system and any problems you may have had or be having but it would be useful to have a general chat about how you feel you are fitting in. Is there anything you would like to discuss?'

'Could we have a chat over lunch about this morning's meeting? I don't think I handled John's outburst very well. In fact I'd like to review team meetings: they seem to have generated into general slanging matches and I'd like to pinpoint where things started going wrong and why.'

'Could you spare 15 minutes tomorrow morning? I want to go through that training plan and check with you which machines you can now operate on your own and which we still need to train you on.'

There is no doubt that effective reviewing will need to take account of such factors as:

• notice and praise of good things;
• supportive and constructive criticism;
• awareness of confidentiality issues;
• openness and honesty;
• tact and sensitivity;
• time allocated to show the value of the process;
• training in communication skills (see Chapter 4).

Appraisal – the process
If an organisation recognises the value of regular review to learn from the past and find new, better, more cost-effective ways of doing things, then the concept of appraisal becomes far less of a threat. Appraisal is simply a planned way of looking at the past, present and future in order to learn and make the most of opportunities. Figure 4.6 indicates the activities and focus of the appraisal process.

Appraisal involves two people (the one carrying out the appraisal – the 'appraiser' – and the one being appraised – the 'appraisee'). However, the process may well involve discussion with other people to check things out, gain further details of particular activities and situations under discussion. As indicated in Figure 4.6, it should include:

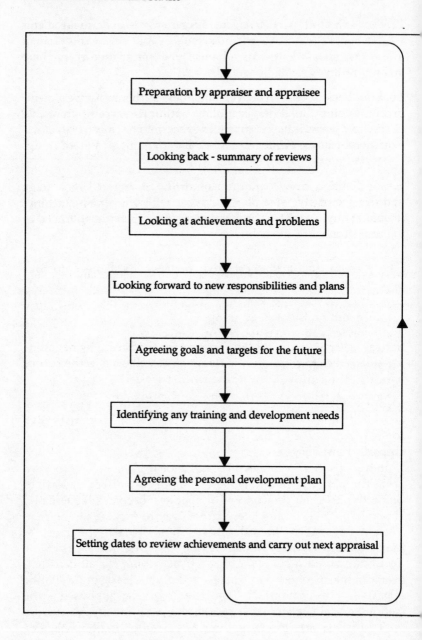

Figure 4.6 *The appraisal process*

Preparation. Both parties need to know what is to be covered and to give some thought to and make some notes about the various areas; this should be discussed and agreed prior to the appraisal and an outline agenda produced.

Looking back. Considering the activities, both achievements and problems, since the last appraisal, or within an agreed time if this is the first appraisal; in particular what targets have been met, exceeded or not met.

Looking at the current situation. Discussing the current role and responsibilities, how the appraisee feels about different aspects and how he or she is using or under-using skills and knowledge, including any current difficulties which might need further training and support to overcome.

Looking forward. Considering the direction and objectives of the business and how the appraisee's role could change and develop; discussing future prospects and new roles and increased responsibilities, particularly identifying new things which the appraisee would like to take on or be considered for.

Setting objectives and targets. Firming up the future by negotiating and agreeing some specific things to be achieved in the future (which will form the basis of the next appraisal).

Identifying training needs. Discussing and completing a personal development plan (see Chapter 2) and considering training needed to improve current role and responsibilities and prepare for changes, new things.

Setting dates. Agreeing times and dates to review progress towards agreed objectives and targets and any other aspects discussed. Agree date of next appraisal.

Making the most of appraisal
To ensure appraisal is rewarding and satisfying for all involved, everyone needs:

- to know the purpose of appraisal;
- to feel it is a **two-way** process, a partnership approach, not something done to someone else;
- to have time to think and plan carefully;

- to be confident that appraisal is an opportunity to exchange views openly and agree future plans;
- to know there will be no sudden 'bombshells': any concerns or problems should be dealt with as they arise, not stored up for the appraisal.

Preparation

As stated, good preparation is vital. Each party should reflect and record thoughts on the key issues to be discussed. You might wish to devise a simple form to support this process as in the example given in Figure 4.7, written for the appraisee, but which could be used equally by the appraiser with slight adaptation. Clearly each party will need to have been given a copy of the other's sheet, in order to make the discussion as effective and useful as possible.

The appraisal interview

Effectively managing the actual appraisal interview of course is crucial; there needs to be:

- adequate time set aside, an appropriate quiet place and no interruptions;
- a disciplined focus on the agreed agenda, concentrating on the job in hand and not being tempted to discuss other work issues;
- good questioning, listening and feedback skills so that both parties feel confident about the discussion;
- a commitment by both to being open and honest;
- recording of the key points, outcomes and agreed points with a copy for each person.

At the end of the interview there should be agreement and understanding of:

- how the appraisee is doing;
- where he or she is going;
- what needs to be improved or developed;
- the personal development plan.

In addition, specific objectives will have been negotiated and agreed. A commonly used reminder about objectives is the word SMART, with objectives being:

Specific – well defined, not woolly or vague.

Measurable – to enable objective review and appraisal of achievement.

Agreed – by both parties to ensure commitment and understanding.

Realistic – they must be challenging, but achievable, to motivate.

Time-related – to give a clear target.

Having carried out an appraisal once and set clear objectives, it becomes much easier to review and discuss objectively the achievements, problems and plans next time!

NB. Pay reviews will inevitably be related to the achievements identified during the appraisal process, but should NOT be part of performance review and appraisal: this, as we have seen, is primarily concerned with helping and discussing with people the ways in which they can best contribute to the success of the business. The value of review and appraisal will be lost if it simply becomes a justification for awarding pay, or not awarding as the case may be.

Building and moving on

The right approach for you

You have now had the chance to review how things are in your organisation with regard to review and appraisal and to study and consider some other ideas and guidelines.

What you decide to do now will obviously depend on where you are now and where you would like to be! Remember, that 'review' and 'appraisal' can be loaded words so it is worth treading slowly and carefully if there are many changes and new things to consider.

If little formal, recognised reviewing currently takes place you may wish to consider:

- trying out some of the ideas in this chapter on yourself first before involving others;
- how to develop some of the crucial skills necessary to

APPRAISAL PREPARATION SHEET
Past and present

What are your current main duties and responsibilities?
For each one, to what extent have you met the requirements?
(A simple scale could be included here).

Duty/responsibility	Requirements		
	Not fully met	Fully met	Exceeded
_____			
_____			
_____			

Looking at the objectives and targets set at the previous appraisal, what have you been able to achieve?

Objective/target	Achieved	Not achieved	Problems
_____			
_____			
_____			

What do you like and feel you tackle most enthusiastically within your current role?

What do you like least and why?

What do you think may have prevented you achieving everything you would have liked to achieve? Identify both your own personal 'barriers' and any constraints in the organisation.

How could your current performance be improved?

The Future

How do you see the business developing in the future?

How would you like your role to develop within this? Think about things in which you would like more or less involvement in the future:

How do you see your career developing both in the short and long term?

Bearing in mind the future, what do you feel are your major strengths and skills, including things you may have developed outside paid work?

What do you feel are your major development needs?

Do you have any suggestions as to areas in which you want further training or experience, and when and how this might take place?

Are there other points you wish to discuss during the appraisal?

Figure 4.7 *Appraisal preparation sheet*

effective review/appraisal, particularly the giving and receiving of feedback;

- gradually introducing a process of review, before even considering the formal appraisal process; starting slowly, perhaps with a small group, or relating to a particular project.

If you feel you and others in your organisation already regularly review some activities and individuals you might look at ways of:

- considering how the current review processes could be improved and further developed;
- identifying who is particularly skilled at reviewing and could possibly take a key role in helping, supporting and training others;
- recording and to some extent formalising the process so that ideas and outcomes of any review are remembered and used;
- applying the current processes and approaches to other activities and people where not covered;
- using some of the suggestions in this chapter and elsewhere in the book, eg, use of learning review logs or developing a mentoring/counselling system (see Chapter 3);
- introducing an appraisal system which would build on the good review practices already in place – considering who might be involved, what further training might be required, when this could happen, how it should work.

If you already have an appraisal system in place you might wish to look at ways of:

- further developing the skills of those involved in carrying out appraisal and considering skills training of all personnel to ensure they have the confidence and competence to make the most of the opportunity;
- changing/improving the procedures, timing and paperwork depending on the outcomes of the stock-take suggested in the first section of this chapter;
- introducing new ideas which may be gleaned from this book, or by discussion with people from other businesses, through groups and other networks (see Chapter 11);

- conducting a more in-depth review of your system if it has been up and running for a while by using an external consultant or attending a training session at a local college or other training provider.

You will find suggestions about all this in the other chapters of this book, particularly the second section which looks at training outside your own business
Whatever you decide to do, it will stand a much better chance of succeeding if:

- managers are enthusiastic, committed and involved;
- the systems are SIMPLE to use;
- people are trained and supported to develop skills;
- the system suits the type of organisation and builds on what is already in place, or manages any changes carefully and gradually;
- everyone can clearly see the purpose and benefits both for themselves and the business.

Benefits of effective review and appraisal
A useful place to start any development is by clearly identifying the benefits. Some of the key benefits of review and appraisal are:

For the individual:
- the opportunity to learn from experiences – and mistakes – in a supportive, constructive way;
- the opportunity to share thoughts and give feedback about the business to other people and thus influence activity and contribute to change and improvement;
- identifying and hopefully removing any barriers to better performance;
- having achievements formally recognised;
- clearing up any problems or worries;
- identifying career opportunities within the business – knowing where one is going;
- agreeing training plans to develop skills and add new ones.

For the business:
- improved commitment and motivation of people and thus

increase of contribution to the growth and success of the business;
- making sure that 'hidden' skills and knowledge are discovered in order to give people the opportunity to contribute as much as possible;
- connecting individual objectives with those of the business and thus maximising the likelihood of achieving business targets;
- encouraging people to work cooperatively together – dealing with problems and issues constructively and developing effective communication/people management skills.

CHAPTER 5
Creating Learning Opportunities

Introduction

In this chapter you will find reference both back to the other chapters in the first half of the book and forward to things which will be explored in more detail in the second half. Opportunities for learning, training and being trained are everywhere – both inside and outside the organisation.

Training can be very costly! You will know this if you have bought in the services of an expert or signed up for a professional development course. However, the cost becomes a worthwhile investment if the training results in clear, measurable improvement in the performance of the individual and the business as a whole. Here, the focus is on cost-effectiveness.

As we have stressed throughout the book so far, making the most of training depends on a number of things such as:

- personal development planning to link individual and business training needs;
- one-to-one support in the workplace to ensure training is relevant and **used** within the job role;
- effective review and appraisal with which people feel confident;
- taking account of new developments in qualifications, recognising the value of the workplace as a learning and training environment.

There are indeed many opportunities for training and learning within your organisation and its sphere of contacts and activity. This chapter should encourage you to think creatively and consider a wide range of ways and resources to use in training your people and enabling them to learn.

Purpose of training	Training method(s)	Comments
Word-processing for receptionists	Local college course	Some useful, but much not relevant. Problems applying to our machines. Two months wait for start of course
Word-processing for new administration assistant	Bought in trainer	Excellent, relevant at time and pace wanted but very expensive for one person

Figure 5.1 *Review of training activities in the past year*

Taking stock

This section will help you consider what current/possible situations exist in your organisation which could provide opportunities for training people. We also suggest a review of how you have approached training in the past: what has been successful and what problems there have been.

Past approaches to training

Start by considering how you have set about training people in any aspect of their job: list as many ways as possible, discuss with others and comment on the effectiveness or otherwise of each. As in previous stocktakes, a simple chart will help you complete this process in a systematic way as in the example in Figure 5.1.

Pass around and invite others to add to your details; you may well have forgotten some of the things you have tried in the past. Other people may well have different perceptions about the effectiveness or value of the training.

How about other possibilities? You may well have considered alternative methods for meeting a training need. Note these and

Name	Preferred approach	Examples/experience

Figure 5.2 *People and their preferred approach to learning*

encourage other people to add to them, commenting on the reasons why you did not pursue other possibilities. You might consider factors such as:

Cost.
Convenience – times, place etc.
Quality of training – past experiences, reputation.
What the individual most wanted or did not want.
Appropriateness – of approach, level, etc.
Familiarity – not feeling confident about a new or different approach.
Any other reasons affecting your choice?

The people in your organisation
Now think about the individuals in your organisation and their personal training and development plans:

Have you given thought to and encouraged individuals to consider different ways in which their learning and training needs could be met?
Do individuals themselves come up with suggestions of appropriate ways to develop new skills and increase their knowledge and understanding?
How well do you know the people in your organisation and the way in which they like to learn and approach new tasks?

You might wish to use the information on learning 'styles' discussed in Chapter 2, Personal Development Planning, to draw up a picture of your people and how they prefer to tackle learning new things (see Figure 5.2).

Current and planned business activities

As part of this stocktake it is worth looking too at what you are currently doing, planning to do and what opportunities these activities might yield for training people in new skills, taking on new responsibilities, acquiring new or increased knowledge, etc. For example, you might have as one of your plans or key business objectives:

Develop export opportunities in France for two current products.

This could give rise to the following **learning** opportunities:

- Visit to potential customers in France to identify opportunities, possible problems and implications – could be 'shadowing' current exporter (non-rival business) on a trip.
- Feasibility project to research into:
  - export rules/procedures
  - packaging needs
  - costs/benefits.
- Hosting visit here of potential customers – organising accommodation and activities.
- Language training: basics for everyone, intensive training for two key sales people.
- Interviewing reps. from other local businesses who currently export to France.
- Attend seminar on exporting at local college.
- Working with external marketing consultant.

Finding out

You have been prompted to take stock of:

- how you currently set about training people;
- business activity/priority and learning opportunity;
- the range of opportunities for learning you have used or thought of using.

Learning opportunities: a list of ideas

Take time now to mull over the following list, particularly those which are not mentioned in your stocktakes. Consider how they could be appropriate for training and encouraging learning in your organisation.

Work-shadowing. One person becomes the 'shadow' of another for a set period of time and follows him/her everywhere: observing, questioning, listening, reflecting, discussing (the concept explored in the book/television series 'Nice Work!').

Projects. Carrying out specific assignments, outside normal work reponsibilities, with set objectives and timescale; often involving investigations, research and development, introducing new/ improved methods, equipment, approaches, etc.

Interviews. Learning from someone, possibly a range of people, inside and outside the organisation, by carrying out planned, in-depth questioning, listening, note-taking, report writing.

Meetings. Attending meetings possibly outside the normal sphere of activity: in other departments, with other people; or outside the business with customers and other business groups to widen scope and understanding of current job and/or the business.

Job swaps. Exchanging work roles and responsibilities with someone else in the organisation to find out about another department/section, understand better the problems, gain new ideas, exchange good practices, etc. Could also take place with another (non-rival) business or customer.

There may be the opportunity to exchange abroad. You might find local schools and colleges have well-established links with their counterparts abroad; one business network we know is currently organising 'Business Exchanges' whereby someone from this country is paired with someone in, say, France and a shadow/swap is arranged. This is not only useful for gaining new ideas and approaches, but also provides an excellent insight into a foreign and possibly different culture: essential for making the most of export opportunities!

Placements and job rotation. Temporary allocation to a different section/job for set period of time; particularly useful for newcomers to the business to gain a useful overview of how all the parts fit!

Group/team-work. Being a member of a team – possibly a project team – undertaking a particular piece of work, learning from other people's way of approaching and tackling tasks.

Learning set. Working in a group – often of business colleagues – which meets regularly for the explicit purpose of sharing and learning from own experience and that of others.

Business contacts. Making the most of contact with suppliers, reps., visitors, customers – discussing and questioning in a planned and systematic way.

Mentor/coach. Working with someone else in a training/learning situation (see Chapter 3, Working one-to-one).

Mistakes and disasters. Instead of sweeping them under the carpet, or ruthlessly dissecting your mistakes or those of others, using them as an opportunity to question, understand and learn.

At the time of writing, there is a series in *The Independent on Sunday* entitled 'My Biggest Mistake' with weekly contributions from successful business men and women who have learned much from a former misjudgement!

This process is helped by using review logs, appraisal, mentoring, etc. to make the most of the learning.

Training resources/other materials. Using videotapes, audiotapes, books, magazines bought or borrowed from libraries, training 'shops', colleges, TECs, etc. as a basis for discussion and exploring new ideas and approaches.

People in one small business we know spend a set hour a week looking at a range of newspapers, discussing local, national and international trends, changes and possible implications for the business in the long term. Where necessary, action points are formalised and followed up.

Using activities outside paid work. Often there are training opportunities in voluntary work, for example:

If you are a school governor, you will have – usually – free or relatively cheap access to a range of courses, materials, etc. many of which have great relevance to a wide range of roles and responsibilities within the business.

Cub/scout leaders, youth leaders, etc. again all have well-organised training.

Samaritans and Relate counsellors, once through the very
rigorous selection procedure, undergo intensive training and
many of the interpersonal and counselling skills are extremely
useful to any business!

Your initial reactions to some of these may well be: 'Well, we do
that already . . .'. Indeed, people may well attend meetings, carry
out interviews and discussions with suppliers and customers, for
example. Is this done *ad hoc* or in a planned way, clearly related to
specific learning objectives as identified and set out in a personal
development plan?

Or you may react: 'That would never work in our business . . .'.
It is wise to be cautious about introducing new ideas, without
careful thought and preparation, but if you have rejected some of
the suggestions from the list above as being unworkable, it is
worth reconsidering. For example, if you feel that 'job swaps'
would cause too much upheaval and time wasting, then you might
consider first, a gradual, systematic development of questioning,
listening, feedback and explaining skills (see Chapter 3); followed
by the introduction of a mentoring system; then using the
mentoring system to support and train people who are carrying
out job swaps or temporary placements.

Making the most of these opportunities
Whichever suggestions you may try to explore and take further,
you will need to be very clear about:

- what learning and/or training is required; as a result of the
  review, appraisal and personal development planning process,
  there needs to be a very clear purpose and specific objectives;
- how this could be done; considering a range of approaches and
  weighing up and discussing the pros and cons of each;
- who could/should be involved; what preparation, training and
  briefing anyone who may be taking on responsibility for training and supporting the learning of another person will need;
- when is the most appropriate time, taking into account the
  various pressure times of the business, or the times where the
  greatest opportunity for learning is to be found.

Planning and preparation, therefore, are as crucial as identifying and creating opportunities for learning, particularly if needs relating both to the individual and the business are to be met.

Making the most of people

Of course it is not always possible to plan and prepare. The unforeseen and unexpected frequently occur. In fact, many successful businesses are the ones which take risks, spot trends and use the opportunities which are suddenly presented. The same is true for successful people: the ones who use their initiative and every situation as an opportunity to learn, grow and develop skills, knowledge and understanding.

If the concept of **personal responsibility** for learning can be encouraged in everyone then you will have a dynamic and healthy atmosphere in your business with the greatest chance of continued success. We have found that the most effective learning and training takes place when people are committed to **self-development**.

The following checklist indicates the characteristics of people who are likely to take responsibility successfully for their own development. You might like to use this as a focus for discussion, or pass around for others to consider.

Building and moving on

What are your reactions to the ideas and suggestions in the previous section? What might be the effects on your business? For example, looking at the characteristics of effective self-developers listed previously, are these the sort of things **you** value and work to encourage in your business? There are some challenges, dangers and many benefits which will need thinking through.

Challenges

Encouraging everyone to learn of course has its dangers – or implications! People will:

- challenge and question old ways of doing things and want to experiment, improve and take risks;
- want and need considerable freedom in which to operate and reject being managed in an authoritarian way.

Checklist of Characteristics of Successful Learners and Self-developers

- They have clear, realistic, personal aims.
- They actively seek out and create opportunities for learning and being trained.
- They use their initiative and work to develop confidence in their own decision-making.
- They recognise the support, help and feedback they need from others and ask for it.
- They frequently appraise themselves against the objectives and targets they have set.
- They view formal appraisal positively and use it as an opportunity to learn and develop and also to negotiate more opportunity and responsibility in the future.
- They make a real effort to establish and maintain good working relationships with as many people as possible.
- They recognise the barriers and blocks to their learning, both personal and organisational, and work to overcome them.
- They recognise their strengths and work to build on them; they recognise their weaknesses and work to overcome them.
- They make room for their own development and work to shape their own job – pushing out the boundaries to take on more.
- They work hard to contribute to teams and groups and to learn from other team members with differing skills, ideas and approaches.
- They consciously use every activity both in and out of paid employment as an opportunity to learn.

How will you and others respond to these and other possible changes? There is clearly a need for **balances**:

- balancing freedom and personal initiative with focus on the business and achievement of business plans and objectives;

- balancing individual learning and training with developing effective teams and work-groups;
- balancing giving direction to and controlling the business with encouraging new ideas and approaches.

Benefits
There are of course many benefits in encouraging and creating learning opportunities and encouraging everyone to see learning and training as crucial for personal and business success. We have found these to be:

- enthusiastic and motivated staff who work well beyond their expected role/job description;
- learning and training carried out very cost-effectively, and very relevant and useful to the business needs;
- people working well together: valuing others and feeling valued themselves and understanding the roles and contributions of other people to the business;
- widening of horizons with people looking up and beyond their own role for new opportunities and experiences, often resulting in a much more positive response to necessary changes;
- the competitiveness of the business: a flow of new ideas and approaches with flexible, adaptable, committed people helps to keep the competitive edge over rivals;
- sharing of the work-load: everyone taking a responsibility for their own learning and for the learning and training of others;
- training and learning woven into the very fabric of the business, not an extra which has to be cut out when funds are low.

Starting points
You might wish to begin by considering:

- to what extent you use or are familiar with the ideas mentioned in the 'Finding Out' section, and what further research and discussion with others you would wish to carry out;
- to what extent you feel the ideas are practicable and would be well received, or what careful preparation you would need to carry out in order to introduce new things gradually;
- who would respond positively to the ideas of self-development

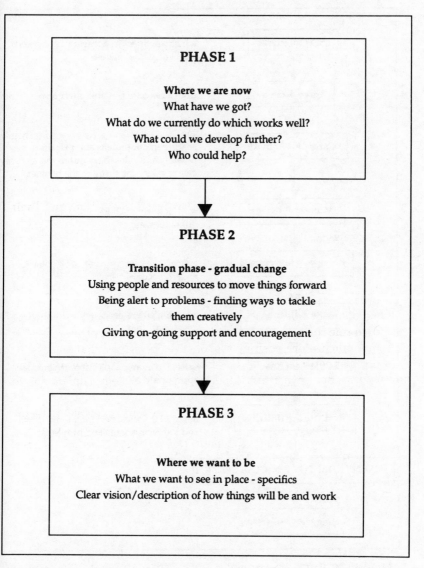

Figure 5.3 *A planned approach to change*

and creating and using learning opportunites of a wide range;
who would be resistant and dig in their heels;
• how you could begin to build on the positive responses to the

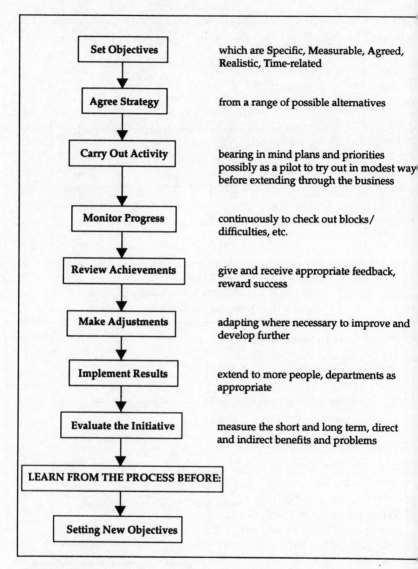

Figure 5.4 *Putting new things into action: a flow chart to show the activities*

above, to develop further what you already have, in order to move forward.

New ideas and approaches involve change. Whatever you decide to do, you will need to manage changes carefully. People tend to be very resistant to change: it can be threatening, frightening and very stressful. Figure 5.3 may help to develop a workable approach by considering the change process in three phases.

Making plans

As well as being aware of these three stages, you may find the flow diagram in Figure 5.4 useful as a guide to the processes and activities involved in putting new things into action.

Finally, here is a checklist which you may wish to use when you are planning to introduce any of the ideas and suggestions we have made for creating and using a wide range of learning opportunities.

Checklist of Issues to be Addressed before Implementing New Ideas	
Issues	*Comments and plans*
Who needs to be committed, consulted and involved in any plans and changes?	
What might be the possible problems and objections?	
What would be the best ways of promoting benefits and minimising objections?	
What on-going support is needed and who could best provide this?	
What are our specific objectives?	
What are the alternative strategies for putting things into action?	

Which would be the best and why?	
What will be the roles and responsibilities to ensure the objectives are met?	

You have now been given a range of ideas to consider and try out as well as some suggestions for implementing your plans in order to make the most of every opportunity for learning and for training people cost-effectively in your organisation. These should result not only in benefits for each individual but, most importantly, give your business a great advantage, increased success and profitability.

CHAPTER 6
National Vocational Qualifications

Introduction

This chapter examines three initials which have in the past appeared baffling to many people involved in business. There are many reasons for this: lack of clear explanation of what National Vocational Qualifications are about, the many jargon words used by people when discussing qualifications, the fact that NVQs are different from the qualifications which you or I may have undertaken. In this chapter we will simplify the qualifications framework so that you can make an informed decision about how you might become involved and how best to give your people credit for what they do. (In Scotland, NVQs are called SVQs, Scottish Vocational Qualifications.)

Taking stock

Being good at the job
What do we mean by saying that someone is 'good at the job'? For many people it is a mixture of skills, knowledge and experience which all adds up to:

- a degree of reliability;
- ability to cope well with pressure;
- consistently high standards of work;
- an in-depth knowledge of the occupation.

Most jobs can be seen in this way: a combination of skills, knowledge and attitudes, and the degree to which people show competence in all three areas usually determine whether we perceive them as performing well in their jobs. The word 'competence' is one which will enter this chapter again and again. It is defined as:

- applying skills and knowledge in real jobs and managing the problems that occur in everyday work;
- performing work activities to the standards required in employment.

Think about your own job.

What knowledge do you need to carry out the many different aspects of the job?
What attitudes have you had to develop?
What are the skills associated with performing your job well?
Which of the above knowledge, skills or attitudes were qualifications for entry into your trade or profession?

Some of the things in your answers were probably learned from a college course or other subsequent training which you have undertaken. Some of them will have been learned from experience of work, some of them learned from experience outside work.

For example, many small to medium sized businesses are owned and managed by people who possess technical skills in their chosen occupational field, and whose business has grown around them, in size, scope, turnover, etc. To manage their businesses effectively many managers have developed new skills, new knowledge and attitudes to cope with the different pressures involved in managing their business.

Refer back to your list. How much of the skills, knowledge and attitudes you possess were learned:
• off-the-job – at school, college, training events?
• on-the-job – through experience?
• outside paid employment?

How much of the skills, knowledge and attitudes which you possess would appear on a certificate?
How would someone interviewing you for a job know that you possessed them?

What do you think would be the benefits of documenting them somehow?

Experiences of gaining qualifications

Many people do not have happy memories of training, trying to gain qualifications, having their skills recognised or seeking employment.

Ask several other people, friends and colleagues, whether any of the following sound familiar:

'I went to college. No, I didn't get the exams – I could do the job, but I could never write essays.'

'I wish I had some kind of record of everything I've learned on training courses to do with my job. All I have got to show is my 3 GCSEs from years ago – I know I should have more than that.'

'I've got loads of experience of working in many different types of business. When I go for job interviews all they ask to see is my qualifications. It does seem unfair.'

'Sometimes you wonder why you bothered. I have got qualifications in banking. I thought about changing career a few years ago and going into estate agency. They told me that I needed an additional GCSE! It seemed crazy after all that training!'

'My qualification was in administration. Yes, I learned a lot, but there is so much more to it when you come to do the real job isn't there?'

'I am the team manager for the local football club/village fete, organiser/in charge of the finances for the local community centre, but no one gives me any credit for that. I know that I am using skills in my leisure activities which could be useful in my job, but I have got nothing to prove it.'

'I find the whole qualification thing really confusing! There seems to be so many different qualifications around, so much overlap and duplication that you wonder whether there could be a simpler way.'

'I left work to bring up a family. Getting back into it was really hard – why couldn't someone have given me some credit for those years – after all, it's managing in its own way!'

'My college course bore no relation at all to my job.'

'I was doing a certificate at college but I had to leave before I completed it as I was ill. All that work – I had nothing to show for it in the end.'

'When you take people on you are never sure of what they can actually do. Someone can look really good on paper but when it comes to the real test – the work itself – can prove hopeless.'

Look at the responses to the statements above. How would you change the system if you could so that everyone got a better deal?

Up to scratch: the standards approach

What are the standards that you expect of yourself in carrying out your job? What standards do you expect of staff?

Make a list using a table like the one shown in Figure 6.1 of the main tasks involved in your job.

By the side of the main tasks break them down into the smaller tasks which you do as part of the main task.

By the side of those add the sort of standards that you would expect of yourself.

How do you know whether your standards are the same as anyone else's?

What are the implications of your standards not being the same as someone else's in a similar position?

Finding out

The old system

Suppose that at 16 years of age you had been given the challenge of hitch-hiking from, say, Land's End to John O'Groats in a certain time. After the constraints of school many 16-year-olds would be excited by that challenge, others would be terrified but most could be persuaded to have a go.

Imagine that instead of the freedom of choice which you had assumed would be yours you discovered that certain rules applied:

you could only accept lifts from cars;

Main task	Smaller tasks	Standards I would expect

Figure 6.1 *Table to analyse tasks and standards*

between Bristol and the Scottish border those cars had to be Fords;
all red cars offering a lift had to be accepted, even if they were not going in the direction that you wanted.

What would have happened to you? You might have been lucky, you might have been hopelessly out of time, you might not have even begun the journey. You might have nearly reached your destination and then because of a break-down 20 miles from the end of the journey have been told that you had failed altogether and had to go back to the beginning.

The old vocational qualifications system in Britain used to be like the story above. There were lots of opportunities and choices, but it was limited by rather silly rules:

• some qualifications could only be obtained by attending a college or other educational institution – like the 'only cars will do' rule in the story above;
• there was a tendency to channel people into doing courses which may not have met their needs – a 'we know what's best

for you' attitude prevailed rather than allowing people to be involved in planning their route for themselves;

• sometimes people got very near to the end of a course only to be unable to finish it for a variety of reasons, from moving area to falling ill, and then they would have to go all the way back to the beginning next time around.

Many 16-year-olds, and indeed older learners, were bewildered and confused by these seemingly meaningless rules. It was time for a change in the qualifications set-up.

The background to the new system

In 1986 the government set up the National Council for Vocational Qualifications (NCVQ). This was charged with the task of pulling together the qualifications system of England, Wales and Northern Ireland. In Scotland, SCOTVEC (Scottish Vocational and Educational Council) was appointed by the Secretary of State for Scotland in 1989 to carry out the same task. They were to do this to overcome the failings of the existing system, outlined above, but also because:

• qualifications were not closely related to the needs of employment;
• the system was over-complicated;
• too few people (only 40 per cent) had vocational qualifications.

There was also a need for higher skills levels in the workforce: increased competition from abroad, the declining numbers of young people entering the labour market and the single European market were just some of the reasons.

So, the task which NCVQ faced was that of making the qualifications framework easily understandable and comprehensive, and one which would enable more people to gain vocational qualifications, rather than actively discouraging or making it difficult for them!

There were, and still are, many vested interests at stake in such a radical shake up. Many of you will be familiar with the examining boards which offer qualifications in vocational subjects:

Royal Society of Arts
City and Guilds
Pitmans
London Chamber of Commerce
Business and Technology Education Council

are just some of the many. You may have also remembered the various training boards, such as the Engineering Industry Training Board, the Construction Industry Training Board, which traditionally managed and offered qualifications in each respective occupational area. The new NVQ framework had to incorporate everything already being done by these examination and training Boards, but impose a new layer of quality assurance onto the existing qualifications, approving qualifications which were being offered and ensuring that they met stringent new standards.

All this had to be achieved while making sure that from then on qualifications in vocational subjects would be firmly rooted in standards of **competence** required by employers. In fact, for the first time, employers were to form groups (called Lead Industry Bodies) for the purpose of getting involved in setting those standards which would then be offered as qualifications by the examining boards. These qualifications were to be called National Vocational Qualifications – the acronym NVQ was born.

NVQs have been in existence since that time, and now most of the framework is in place. They are offered in Levels to indicate the extent of a person's competence in that occupational area:

Level I   is foundation level, dealing with work activities which are routine or predictable.

Level II   is more demanding, dealing with work activities which involve greater responsibility.

Level III   is more complex, dealing with non-routine activities; supervisory duties may be included at this level.

Level IV   is supervisory or management level, dealing with technical or professional work activities.

Level V   the NCVQ is currently undertaking further development work in this area.

The difference between old style qualifications and new NVQs is shown in Figure 6.2.

Traditional qualifications have been:	NVQs are:
learned through courses	standards-based
created from an academic syllabus	derived from industry standards
learned in a specific way	any pace, length of study
concerned with pre-entry requirements	without specific pre-entry requirements
college-based	workplace-based
only pass or fail	continuous assessment
a qualification or not	an accumulation of competences
concerned with skills and knowledge	concerned with skills, knowledge and their application

Figure 6.2 *Differences between traditional qualifications and NVQs*

What are the benefits of NVQs?

If you refer back to the 'Taking Stock' activities at the beginning of this chapter you will remember the sort of things which were wrong with the way qualifications were structured in the past. This is not to say that those qualifications in themselves were not of value; of course they were. There are, however, better ways of organising things. The benefits of the approach that the NCVQ has taken are that NVQs:

- are about showing competence – what people can do – so there is no insistence on the qualification being gained in any

particular way. What matters is not how you got the qualification, but that you are qualified;
- do not mean jumping through hoops. If you can already perform competently then you do not have to sit and learn how to do it all over again. Imagine the possibilities of this! You and your staff could gain formal recognition through qualifications for **what you can prove that you can do competently already**;
- are relevant to employment and recognise real work ability;
- provide motivation for employees who can see how they relate to their jobs and give credit where credit is due;
- do not put up barriers, like age, duration of course, place of attendance for learning, but test outcomes.

What do NVQs look like?
NVQs are made up of standards of competence. As we have said before, this means that candidates must demonstrate that they can do things, consistently to standards **in the workplace**.

NVQs are made up of the components shown in Figure 6.3. Beware of the jargon in the figures; we thought it helpful to include so that when you come across an NVQ being followed by one of your members of staff you recognise it, but we have added our own explanation of what those terms really mean.

Assessing NVQs
As you can see from the above, work-related standards are an important part of NVQs. This means that in order to obtain an NVQ a person must show that he or she can consistently apply skills and knowledge in the workplace, or in a situation which provides a realistic simulation of the workplace. This is very new – as we have mentioned, qualifications were based on traditional examinations or skills tests. To insist on assessment taking place at work is a huge change in the nature of qualifications, and one which has major implications for every employer in the country.

When being assessed for an NVQ a person will have to provide **evidence** or proof of competence, which can be given in a number of different ways, depending on what the NVQ specifies. The evidence could be:

• from observing someone in the workplace;
• from looking at examples of someone's work in the workplace;

An NVQ is made up of:

Title of Qualification	Unit of Competence	Elements with Performance Criteria
which means:		
the examining board the occupational area the level of qualification	the main task areas	smaller task areas and the standards which must be met
for example,		
RSA Business Administration Level II	Filing	Carries out routine alphabetical filing: in alpha order files labelled paper secure papers tidy

Figure 6.3 *The components of an NVQ*

• from skills tests in the workplace;

and/or from:

• oral questioning;
• written answers to questioning;

and/or from:

• evidence from things which someone has done in the past.

How does all this apply to me?
There are two main ways in which you might become involved with National Vocational Qualifications.

1. Working with a training provider or college
Let us suppose that one of your team is pursuing, say, a secretarial qualification through a local college or training provider, which you have supported and encouraged. The qualification for which he or she is aiming is likely to be an NVQ, through one of the examining boards (probably RSA, BTEC, London Chamber of Commerce or Pitmans). She or he will have to provide proof of competence against the various components of that qualification, eg, filing, typing, organising meetings, etc. to the standards laid down by the qualification.

The college or training provider will no doubt want to discuss with you or the person's supervisor the candidate's progress, and whether or not he or she is competent.

Your involvement:

- your skills, or the skills of someone else in your organisation, will be called upon to take a part in the assessment of the workplace evidence as outlined in the list above;
- most examining boards now require those people involved in assessment of candidates to have obtained some kind of assessor qualification, and so it is likely that formal assessing will be done by the college/training provider, who may need to come into your workplace to observe the candidate;
- your comments and opinions about the candidate's performance will be asked for by that assessor.

2. Operating your own NVQ programme(s)
If you have a regular number of staff undertaking qualifications, as would, for example, a busy hairdressing studio with several staff members being trained up in a year, it might be advantageous to you to run your own NVQ programme. Many large companies already do this. You would, in other words, be cutting out the 'middle person', and as in every occasion where this happens, would be much more responsible for the whole operation. In this case your involvement would be much more direct.

Your involvement:

- you would be organising and managing the training programmes of the staff/trainees in question;

- either you or one of your staff would be directly responsible for assessing the candidate's progress;
- you would also be involved in liaising with the examining board when your candidates were ready to apply for their certificates, so that the board could check out whether standards had been maintained.

Now let's see how you might go about organising all this.

Building and moving on

Look back at the 'Taking Stock' section of this chapter. Compare your responses to the statements and questions about qualifications with the information which we have given you in the last section.

What is your immediate reaction to the idea of NVQs?
Which staff do you think might be interested in training for further qualifications?
Which staff do you think have got skills and knowledge already in their occupational areas which have never received any recognition? These staff might be able to gain an NVQ without carrying out any extra learning.
What do you think would be the benefits for your business in either getting involved yourself or encouraging staff to undertake NVQs?
To what extent would you get involved? (In conjunction with a college/training provider, or on your own account?)
What would be the advantages and disadvantages of each approach?
What would be the implications in terms of time/money?

Getting started
You will need to decide which of the approaches you are going to take, as outlined above:

1. Getting involved through a local college/training provider.
2. Managing your own training programmes by liaising with an examinations board.

1. Partnership approach with a local college/training provider
If you have not had any involvement with qualifications before it may be that you wish to 'dip your toe in the water' by contracting with a training provider. This would give you the experience of getting to grips with training, assessing and submitting candidates for certification without too much trouble. See Chapter 8 on local training providers for more information on how to make the most of their services. As we say in Chapter 9 on choosing and using a consultant, using external advisors can be an excellent source of learning, and so taking this first approach could provide you with a lot of valuable information about the skills associated with operating NVQs within your business.

2. Going it alone
If you decide that the size of your business, your commitment to training and qualifications and the number of people who are seeking qualifications merits it, you can contact the examining boards directly. Some of the main ones are listed in the Appendix at the back of this book, but there are many more, and you might find that your particular occupational area is not represented in this list. Your local Training and Enterprise Council or college should be able to provide you with the address of the examining board which represents your occupational area.

Offering NVQs: what will it entail?
The examining boards will want to see evidence that you can:

- cope with training – that your staff who will be responsible for supervising are well qualified in their occupational area; some boards might look for extra training qualifications;
- cope with assessment – most boards look for qualified assessors nowadays; they will usually offer their own training (which you will have to pay for) to support this;
- ensure that trainees can learn what they need to meet all the competences laid down in the NVQ, to the standards expected; they will ask you how this is going to be done and want to feel sure that real training will be happening on the job;
- provide the background knowledge which might be required in the NVQ – in some cases there are questions about the occupational area which trainees have to answer; if you cannot

provide this they will want to be sure that you will arrange for trainees to have access to someone/something which can (college training for example);
- review your training provision – they will want to see evidence that this will be done;
- provide the necessary equipment and resources for the trainees to learn the skills involved in the NVQ; for example, if operating a milling machine is part of an engineering NVQ it would be no good telling the board that you do not have this equipment and cannot, therefore, offer training in that area unless you could arrange for trainees to learn that skill somewhere else.

Assessment: the implications
You would need to give this careful thought. Assessment can be a time-consuming business.

> How many people would be involved in assessment if you decided to become involved with NVQs?
> Who possesses the necessary skills to make the best assessors, and would be willing to take a qualification to become approved as one?
> How would you ensure that someone's role as a work-place assessor was recognised – formally, informally; through extra pay; extra time given?
> How would you cope with the possible problems of people assessing others on the same level as themselves? You might need to do this in order to spread the load rather than having just one person assessing.

Final thoughts
If all this has been quite new to you then take heart from the fact that the majority of employers in this country are not familiar with the new qualifications structure. For most people it has passed by quite unnoticed.

If you are still unsure about whether the subject of qualifications has anything to do with your business take a look at Chapter 10 on Training and Enterprise Councils, particularly the section on 'Investors in People', the national award for businesses which invest in training and development. The number of people who possess qualifications, and have been supported in obtaining them by you, is certainly a mark of a quality business in the same way that the now much-publicised BS5750 is a mark of a business which meets certain quality standards in its operating systems. Showing your commitment by ensuring that staff gain accreditation for their work is very good evidence that your company is really investing in people, and that in turn is good PR for your business.

Remember, by becoming involved with qualifications you are giving formal recognition to things which probably exist in your company at present:

- people's occupational skills;
- people's skills as trainers and assessors;
- your organisation's commitment to staff development and training.

Section II Looking Outside Your Business

Introduction to Section II

We have looked in Section I at how to make the most of your business starting from the inside. We have suggested building upon what already takes place within it and of developing new strategies for improving opportunities for learning for everyone involved in the business.

In Section II we will concentrate upon a range of organisations and services which exist outside your business. These should be able to help you develop training opportunities for your staff.

There are good reasons for using outside contractors to support training and development for your business. Looking outside can stop you becoming out of touch and offers fresh ideas and approaches. Like any other goods or services which you purchase, however, there are some common sense tips which will help you get the most from outside suppliers.

- Be clear about what exactly you need and what the outcomes of the training service which you are going to purchase should be. What do you want to happen as a result of using outside expertise?
- Use the same quality checks as you would on any other supplier; take time initially to ensure that the quality of what is being offered meets your needs.
- Shop around to ensure that you feel happy with the cost of what is being offered. Remember that just as the lowest price might not the most cost-effective in the long run, so a high price does not guarantee that you will get what you need.
- Support the training which you have decided to buy in by ensuring that you make conditions right in the business for

people to practise their newly acquired skills.
• Monitor and evaluate the usefulness of the service which is being provided. Remember, you are paying for the service so make sure that you make the most of it.

We hope that you will find Section II a useful and informative balance to Section I.

CHAPTER 7
Using Local Colleges

Introduction

Wherever you live in Great Britain, in the nearest good-sized town there is likely to be a college of further education. Once designated the local 'tech', for technical college, it was the place where:

- apprentices did their day-release courses;
- employed adults improved their prospects by attending night school;
- young people, disenchanted with school, could attend on a full-time or part-time basis to pick up extra 'O' levels or follow 'A' level courses or gain a range of vocational qualifications;
- anyone could go for a range of sport and leisure activities and classes.

Indeed today if you wish to gain, for example, 'A' level English or a City and Guilds qualification in carpentry and joinery or acquire expertise in Indian cookery, then your local college would probably meet your needs.

However, as in all areas of education, times are changing. During the past decade there has been a revolution in many colleges with new products, new services and new approaches aimed at new markets.

Marketing, customers, quality, flexibility, diversity, commercial viability and the business community are becoming increasingly crucial concerns. It is planned that by mid-1993 colleges will cease being controlled by local authorities and that as independent organisations will be in the competitive market-place.

In this chapter we hope to encourage you to look afresh at your local college(s), consider what is on offer and how you might make the most of current provision and influence and encourage them to respond to your needs.

Taking stock

Local colleges and your experiences
So what is the current situation, relationship, contact between your local college(s) and your business? Use the following questions to check out what is happening and reflect on your experiences, impressions, feelings and those of other people.

Obviously, if you live or work in a very rural area, the choice of convenient college may be limited. It is worth, wherever possible, taking stock of two or three: the approach, range of products and services may differ. Some have radically changed the way they work, others are evolving and moving more slowly.

Which are your nearest (say) three colleges of further education?

What do you know and what experience have you and other people in your company, and business networks had of local colleges and the quality and range of their provision?

Completing and passing round to as many people as possible the kind of table shown in Figure 7.1 will help draw together a picture.

Having invited as many people as possible to note their experiences and observations, assess:

What are the general patterns?

What are seen to have been the useful experiences and positive responses?

What have been the problems and unsatisfactory experiences and why?

Do there appear to have been any changes in provision and/or people's experiences over a period of time?

Are these positive or negative? Why?

This should have given you a general impression about the college and its activity from the contacts people have had or which are

Name of college:	
Contact/experience (details of what done, when, etc.)	Comments (about specific courses, etc. and the college generally)

Figure 7.1 *An analysis of contacts with a local college*

current. Of course these contacts might have been long courses, a short-lived enquiry, work-related, leisure, sport, etc.

It would obviously be worth exploring in some detail the services colleges provide specifically for businesses and how they approach the business market.

Incidentally, this kind of research activity could form the basis of an excellent learning opportunity for a member of your staff (see Chapter 5, Creating Learning Opportunities). Perhaps a young person, or someone you have identified as being suitable to take on some staff training and development responsibility, could carry it out. In fact, many of the 'Taking Stock' activities provide opportunities for interesting projects.

There are a number of strategies which could be used to find out about college services for the business market. These could include:

- telephone enquiries – both general and specific;
- letters of enquiry;
- visits – both with and without prior appointments;

- studying the prospectus and promotional literature;
- attending open days, presentations, career and training conventions, etc.;
- interviews with college personnel – having previously identified people with responsibility for services to business;
- looking at the college profile and involvement in the business community – contacts with individual companies and business networks;
- looking at the college marketing strategy and efforts – advertisements, features in local and business press, mailshots and information leaflets, visits by college staff to business, etc.

Having collected and sorted the results of your research, you should be in a good position to judge whether or not your local college is likely to be able to meet your needs, or at least interested in responding to requests. We have found that responsive, effective and business oriented colleges are likely to have most of the features on the following checklist.

Checklist for Assessing Your Local College/s

- There are car-parking facilities for visitors and/or arrangements or suggestions for use of convenient public car parks.
- There is a welcoming, clearly sign-posted reception, with maps or diagrams of the college to help the visitor who is not a regular customer; an efficient, business-like welcome from the receptionist who is clearly well-informed about the college activities and the roles and responsibilities of those within it.
- Telephone enquiries are handled efficiently, with the caller passed to an appropriate person. Any unresolved query is followed up as soon as possible by a named person; ie, the college is clearly geared up to deal with enquiries from potential business customers at any time of the year.
- From the advertising and information details, it is evident that market research has been carried out to identify the needs of the business market. Training courses on offer relate to the issues currently facing you and your business.

- There is an advice and counselling service to enable business clients to discuss their needs and negotiate appropriate provision to meet these.
- Flexibility is built into all training offered: courses, seminars, etc. can be negotiated at times and places to suit. The college has clearly moved away from the traditional 'academic year' with training provision starting in September and finishing in June: there is clear evidence of being 'open all hours'!
- There is a good range of up-to-date training resources and materials related to business: video and audio tapes, open learning materials and training packages, computer-based training activities which are used by college staff and available for customers to use.
- A consultancy service is available, whereby businesses have access to specialists to discuss particular problems or who are available to come and work on a project basis within the business.
- A customised training service is available, whereby the college will plan, develop and deliver training tailored to meet the particular needs of the business. This is available either in the college or in the company.
- There is clear evidence that college staff are encouraged to forge links with businesses, keep up-to-date with latest issues, approaches and technology. Where necessary the college contracts with external specialists to ensure quality provision.
- There is a clear commitment to quality: to identify and meet customer needs, to ensure a professional approach to training with first-class resources and materials, to review and check how things are going and to carry out with the customer a final evaluation. There are positive attempts to seek out and respond immediately to feedback from the customer.

So how does your local college measure up?

Before you rush to telephone the college either to make the most of the wonderful range of facilities and training for businesses it has to offer, or, alternatively to complain about the lack of them, it is worth considering what you do actually want and expect!

What do you and others see as the role of the local college in meeting the needs of small and medium sized businesses and the staff with them?

What products and services do you particularly want?

What is important to you in considering how your needs should be met?

When and where do you want college services to be available?

What particular resources and equipment would you expect them to have to meet the needs of your business?

What particular experience and expertise do you want from college people with whom you may negotiate and work?

Finding out

From the previous section you should have a good idea of the current situation in your local college or colleges. You will have been prompted to think about your needs and will probably have formed a judgement on how far the college is likely to be able to meet them effectively and efficiently.

In this section there is information about the very comprehensive range of products and services on offer. You will be lucky to find one local college carrying out all of the following, but it will give you some idea of what you could expect or ask for.

This list should be very useful when discussing personal action plans with people in your business and it may well prompt a number of ideas which could result in useful contacts and partnerships being formed with college staff.

Local colleges: products and services

Degree courses. Many colleges of further education now work closely with institutions of higher education – polytechnics and universities – to offer degree-level courses, or modules towards degrees.

GCSE, 'A' Level and AS Level. Colleges continue to provide traditional educational qualifications for young people (16 plus) who may prefer college to staying on at school or for older people who wish to increase their qualifications. Often courses can be followed during the day or the evening and sometimes by distance learning, in your own home.

Alternatives to 'A' Level. Colleges also offer alternative routes to higher education; for example, a two-year BTEC national course can be followed instead of or sometimes in conjunction with 'A' levels to gain access to degree courses.

Job skills and vocational training. Colleges continue to offer a full range of vocational training: building trades, engineering, electronics, hairdressing, care, catering, office skills, design, leisure and tourism, etc. With the introduction of NVQs (see Chapter 6) however, there has been increased emphasis on work experience, work placements, and assessment in the workplace or under work conditions.

Professional courses. As well as a very wide range of vocational training aimed at preparing young people to enter paid work, or re-skilling and up-skilling older people, there is often a range of professional qualifications for training in supervisory skills, management, accountancy, teaching and training, for example. If you are interested in becoming more involved in NVQs and running your own staff training programmes leading to qualifications, colleges often offer assessor training for particular NVQs and vocational areas.

Business training Most colleges now offer courses and other training specifically for businesses. These might include a short course programme of half, one or two day courses on a range of topics such as: exporting, first aid, health and safety, business planning, recruitment and selection of staff, appraisal, information technology, employment law, equal opportunities, marketing, quality assurance, etc.

There may be individual seminars where someone with particular expertise or experience runs the session; for example a BS5750 (the British Standard for quality systems) assessor may run an introductory seminar to explain the standard, the benefits and how to obtain it.

It should be noted that often many courses and seminars for small businesses are subsidised by the local TEC (see Chapter 10).

For key local and national issues, conferences or conventions may be held on, for example, 1992, Europe and the Implications for Business, Training and Career Development.

Some colleges host business clubs where members meet perhaps one evening a month to discuss particular issues or problems, exchange ideas, make contacts and possibly to listen to a guest speaker.

Colleges run update courses as regulations or procedures change, for example on new electrical wiring regulations, or COSHH – Control of Substances Hazardous to Health, or food hygiene regulations.

There may be a business counselling service whereby businesses have access to specialist advice and help. This may result in negotiating further training or consultancy support in the workplace. In fact many colleges are now geared up to work with local businesses to provide customised training – designing and delivering training to meet the needs of a particular business. This might take place in the college or on the business premises, for example, intensive language training for a business wishing to export to a particular country or specific computer software training.

Some colleges have well-established links with the business community and have for many years offered technical support services and research and development facilities. An engineering company, for example, may consider investing in expensive new computerised equipment. A well-equipped local college will enable an in-depth scrutiny of the proposed new equipment, with some 'hands-on' experience and trials before deciding on a purchase. New systems and product trials can be tested in a college workshop, perhaps as a student project before going 'live' in the workplace. Indeed business problem-solving is often offered: students on management, business and technical courses need real-life case studies if their training is to be relevant.

Business start up training. Many colleges offer training programmes for people wishing to start their own business. These will cover the knowledge and skills needed to research and develop a business idea and take the learner through all the stages necessary, as well as offering support and advice on grants, premises, etc.

Recruitment services. Colleges are often very good starting points if you are looking for new staff. As well as containing young people finishing full-time courses who are seeking employment, many colleges are managing agents for Youth Training and Employment Training. You can work with college staff to recruit and select the new staff you need and there will often be a subsidy for continuing their training. This takes much of the worry and hassle out of doing it all yourself.

Employment services. For the unemployed, too, there are often many services within the local college. Many run job clubs to offer support and advice in job hunting and there is usually a personal and careers counselling service to enable individuals to make the most of what is on offer. For women, in particular, who may have had a career break, there are introductory and refresher courses to enable skills to be updated and new directions considered.

Access courses. Before individuals commit themselves to a demanding programme of training, it is advisable to undergo careful preparation. Often colleges will offer study skills and other introductory courses, designed to give new students of all ages confidence in tackling learning; or they may offer tasters to enable individuals to try out courses before making firm commitments.

Basic skills. The majority of colleges offer literacy and numeracy support, often in informal drop-in workshops.

Adult education programme. There is usually still a wide range of adult leisure and interest courses. There are many thriving businesses which started up as the result of a hobby being developed!

Other services and resources. In addition to the above, you can expect to find such facilities as a crèche, library and resource centre, information centre, leisure and sport facilities, conference and seminar facilities.

Prior learning assessment and accreditation. Some colleges are beginning to develop an APL (Accreditation of Prior Learning) centre where you may go and discuss with a trained person all the skills, knowledge and experience you have gained through life – both in and out of paid work. Arrangements can be made for these to be assessed, evidenced and finally accredited. Thus you may gain a qualification with little or no further training. This process can give you entry onto higher-level training programmes.

Colleges: the market and the approach

From the above list, it should be obvious that the potential market for the college and its products and service is all-encompassing. Indeed many colleges use messages such as: 'Serving the Whole Community'; 'Your Local College – whether you are 6 or 60 plus'. These are not advertising slogans: we do know of colleges where:

- there are activities at weekends and in the holidays for young children;
- you can take almost any GCSE or 'A' level by home study with tutorial support or using extensive information technology and library facilities at any time of the year;
- there are pre-retirement courses to make the most of new freedom;
- businesses are offered a full range of advice and consultancy;
- anyone can make a start on a new career.

We know too where the provision is considerably less extensive!

As well as developing a wide range of products and services for an equally wide-ranging market, many colleges have radically changed the way they operate. The traditional college clung very much to the academic year, with set courses and timetables. Some have swept these away; others have begun to adapt and make them more flexible. They are gradually becoming more customer-oriented: the starting point is the individual customer and his/her needs. The education/training package is negotiated and planned to meet these needs. In the past, and still in the present in some colleges, there is a course list from which individuals can choose. Some of the other, newer approaches are:

- distance/correspondence learning (often with tutorial support);
- open/flexible learning – time and place negotiable;
- computer-assisted learning;
- drop-in workshops;
- personal tutor to support self-directed learning;
- learning sets or groups with or without tutor support;
- customised training – designed to the customer's specification;
- collaborative training with businesses;
- in-house training – on the customer's premises;
- modular approach with credits to enable gradual collection for the award of a qualification.

As with all changes and developments, the success and enthusiasm will vary. But **you** as a current or potential customer have the opportunity, together with your business colleagues, to influence and affect the provision made by **your** local college. If you do not feel it is ready, willing and able to meet all your needs, you will have to work with others to push for what you need and deserve. Even if your local college is very forward-looking and responsive to the needs of the business community, there are a number of things which you need to do to make sure you make the most of any training provided by the college.

Building and moving on

So far in this chapter we have encouraged you to find out about what your local colleges have to offer, to consider what you expect of the provision and to update yourself on the wide range of possible products and services and approaches.

This last section is very much how to make the most of your college. There are two main ways in which you as a business can do this:

1. Act as a catalyst for change yourself to ensure your needs are met.
   Develop as many contacts and links as possible and use every opportunity to offer suggestions, influence, make requests, offer services and facilities, give feedback, etc. – anything to encourage a response to your needs. You may need to be persistent and it will help if you have support (see Chapter 11, Networks and Partnerships).
2. Be a model of good practice yourself to gain maximum benefit from any college provision even if it does not yet meet your requirements fully.
   If you have tackled positively many of the ideas in the first section of the book – on looking in at your own business – then you are likely to make the most of the opportunities 'outside'.

Ideas for making the most of your local college

- Remember you are a potential customer and the college is a potential supplier of training and related services. It will help if

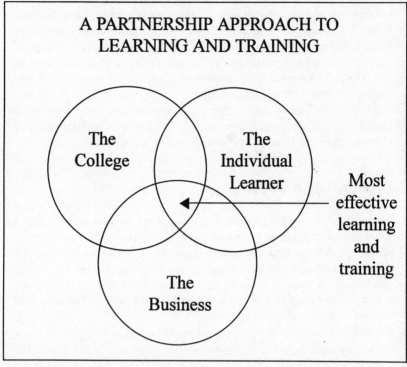

Figure 7.2 *Effective partnerships: the college, the individual learner and the business all working together*

you know what you want and take the time to communicate this clearly.
- Make contacts: go to open days and other events; invite college staff into your company; find out about and get involved in any networks and business clubs arranged by the college and if they do not meet your needs try and influence them; offer work experience and training places to students and other trainees; look for opportunities for collaborative ventures with the college.
- Use your own business networks to plan cost-effective training: three, four or more small businesses could share the expense of a college course designed to meet their particular needs, run at a time and place convenient to them AND have enough participants to make it viable.

- Be creative! We have seen very effective exchange systems working: a member of the college coming in to a business to work with people, carry out some training; an employee of the business running a session, being a guest speaker at the college. There are many opportunities for swapping, with great benefits both to business and college (see Chapter 11, Networks and Partnerships, for further ideas.)
- Plan well in advance the training you will be needing over the coming year: refer to Chapter 1 to support this process and negotiate with the college. You might also wish to discuss your training needs with other training providers (see Chapters 8 and 9 on using training providers and consultants) – healthy competition will not do colleges any harm!
- Work with college staff to agree the objectives and details of any training to be provided to ensure the training is relevant and delivered in the most appropriate way.
- Make sure you have things in place in your own company before agreeing any training and support from outside. The individuals who will be undergoing the training need to know why they are to be trained and what is expected of them. Hopefully they will have negotiated all this as part of the personal development planning and appraisal process. People should never just be 'sent on courses', if you really want them to be committed to their learning and development!
- Consider a mentor system to help those undergoing training courses make the most of new ideas and experiences and plan how best to **use** their learning for the benefit of the business.
- Consider too the implications for the business and the changes which may need to be made. There is nothing more soul destroying than for someone to attend a useful and interesting course and then find that there is no opportunity or encouragement to put new ideas and approaches into practice. It is one of the quickest ways of destroying motivation!
- Take time to review and evaluate the training with college staff and learners. If things are not going well, discuss this with the college as soon as possible so that adjustments can be made. Give feedback and suggestions to the college staff – they need to know what works and what needs changing if they are to meet the needs of their customers.
- Think in terms of **partnerships** (see Figure 7.2). We have found that the best training occurs when the college, the individual

learner and his or her company are **all involved and all take responsibility for all stages of the training,** from the initial negotiating through planning, carrying out, reviewing and evaluating. It is often helpful to discuss and set down formally plans and objectives in the form of a 'contract' at the beginning of any programme of training. In this way everyone is clear about what is expected and the chances of misunderstandings and mismatches are minimised.

CHAPTER 8
Using Local Training Providers

Introduction

Until fairly recently in the history of education and training, people obtained vocational qualifications in the main at technical colleges, which then became known as colleges of further education. Nowadays the picture is much wider, with a variety of different providers, even schools, offering vocational qualifications. This chapter looks at the role of government-funded training providers, explains what they do and why they were set up. It explores whether you might benefit from their services.

Taking stock

The local training scene

What do you know about training organisations?
Who runs them and how much do you know about what they do?

Try asking yourself and your colleagues the following questions to check out your knowledge of local training provision:

Have you had dealings with training providers? If so, what were your experiences?
Have you ever heard of YT?
Have you ever heard of ET or AT?
Have you ever taken on a trainee under the Youth Training Scheme, or Employment Training?

What do the responses tell you about the image of training in this country? Often people have quite jaundiced opinions of local training schemes, and will remind you of the long-gone days of work experience programmes where trainees were used as 'cheap labour'. This is undoubtedly founded on fact, for indeed there were many things wrong with the fore-runners of the training programmes which exist today. It takes an awful long time before the bad news stories fade into the past. Today there are plenty of excellent organisations providing quality training for excellent trainees, so do not let this put you off! However, you still need to evaluate critically what these businesses are doing so that you can decide for yourself whether you could make use of their services.

Let us investigate the local training scene a little more closely. See how far you can answer the following questions:

How do local businesses train their staff? Like, for example
- hairdressers
- engineering firms
- building firms
- electricians
- accountants
- computer programmers.

Who are your local training providers?
What training do they offer?
Have you ever needed advice or help with setting up new training programmes for your staff?
Have you ever needed help with recruitment and selection?

If the answer to most of these is, 'I don't know', then you may be missing out on opportunities for your business which might provide you with cost-effective methods for recruitment and training of new staff.

The following background information will give you a starting point upon which to begin to form some opinions.

Finding out

New Training Initiative: the background
In 1981 a White Paper was published entitled *The New Training Initiative* (NTI) which proposed three major objectives. These were:

- We must develop skills training including apprenticeship in such a way as to enable young people entering at different ages and with different educational attainments to acquire agreed standards of skill appropriate to the jobs available and to provide them with a basis for progression through further learning.
- We must move towards a position where all young people under the age of 18 have the opportunity either of continuing in full-time education or of entering a period of planned work experience combined with work-related training and education.
- We must open up widespread opportunities for adults, whether employed, unemployed or returning to work, to acquire, increase or update their skills and knowledge during the course of their working lives.

This document signalled the coming of major changes in vocational training. These objectives were not realised for several years. Beneath the wordy sentences the ideas are quite simple:

- The first objective was realised with the re-design of the qualifications system. Chapter 6, on National Vocational Qualifications, explains these changes.
- The second objective became what we now know as the Youth Training Scheme.
- The third objective focused on adults and a variety of training programmes for adults have been the result.

As a result of the second objective, a one-year Youth Training Scheme was launched in 1983, just two years after the NTI. It was the first attempt at starting to meet the increasing needs of employers for better skilled young people entering the labour market.

This was the background to the development of what we now know as youth and adult training. There have been various titles to these programmes over the years, and because of this the picture can seem confusing. These are just some of them:

YTS – Youth Training Scheme: a one- and two-year programme for 16–18-year-olds to combine work experience with day-release training.
JTS – Job Training Scheme: based on YTS, but for adults.

CP – Community Programme: a back-to-work work experience scheme for adults; no mandatory training.

YT – Youth Training: a more flexible version of the original YTS; day-release not mandatory, but there must be provision of a structured training programme with an employer.

ET – Employment Training (often referred to as AT – adult training): a variety of flexible training packages for adults.

Youth and adult training: the initials YT and ET have, in some cases, been dropped, so that training for young people and adults is seen as a normal part of any job and not something separate from it.

The initials may have changed, but the principle of a structured training programme which combines work with learning is still evident in youth and adult training programmes today.

It was obvious that new organisations would have to be formed to manage these new training schemes. The Government department responsible was then the Manpower Services Commission (the MSC) which licensed organisations to run the training programmes. The organisations which put themselves forward were made up in a variety of different ways:

some were backed by Chambers of Commerce;
some were part of Local Authority divisions;
some were based within colleges;
some were in-company schemes (usually large companies);
some were a mixture of some or all of the above;
some were private companies set up specifically for this reason.

The organisations became known as 'managing agents'. Their task was to organise training for young people through work experience with employers and off-the-job training which they provided themselves or which a college undertook. They received a management fee plus an allowance per trainee for running the scheme. Employers were asked to contribute to the cost of training the young people.

The training programmes which managing agents provided had to show certain characteristics. The MSC insisted that:

• formal off-the-job training was combined with work experience;

- trainees were equipped with key skills such as communication, numeracy, computer literacy;
- trainees were given opportunities to develop 'personal effectiveness' – in other words, skills which would stand them in good stead for life, such as teamwork, initiative, responsibility;
- trainees were encouraged to think broadly about how the skills which they were learning could be used in other occupational areas – this was to ensure that young people who would probably face many changes of job/career were equipped to cope.

Today this foundation still underlies youth and adult training provision, but it is no longer the mandatory requirement that it once was. Companies and training providers receiving government funding to provide youth and/or adult training can be fairly flexible as to the make-up of training programmes. For example, as long as it can be demonstrated clearly that all the training required is being given on the employer's premises, a training provider would not necessarily insist on day-release training. What does matter is the outcome of a trainee working with an employer. The training providers are judged on:

- achievement of National Vocational Qualifications;
- the trainee becoming employed or entering education.

The way in which training providers had traditionally worked changed with the coming of the Training and Enterprise Councils (TECs). The responsibility for youth and adult training passed into TEC control (see Chapter 10 for more on this) and many managing agents found themselves operating to new guidelines, in a more aggressive market. There was a general shake-up, and those training organisations which survived began to be more commercial and less reliant on government funding than in the old days.

Today many training providers are rather like small private colleges, offering supervisory and management training as well as traditional skills training. Youth and adult training is more flexible, and the emphasis for training providers is on ensuring jobs with training, rather than training with work experience. Indeed, as outlined above, training providers who are operating with some government funding are judged by the TECs on how many people have gained full-time employment, and how many have gained qualifications, and their continued funding often depends upon this.

Where do I fit in?

You could use the services of local training providers in a number of ways:

- as advisers/consultants to assist you with specific training requirements, such as developing a training plan for all your staff or identifying staff training needs;
- as providers of business training (some, not all, will offer this);
- as providers of employees and trainees for your business.

If you are going to use a local training provider for any of the above you will want to be sure that you are going to get the best possible service cost-effectively. In Chapters 7 and 9 on using local colleges and consultants, we have addressed some of the issues which you need to think about before deciding on spending money on consultancy or training courses. Refer to these chapters if you are interested in using your local training provider in the first two ways outlined in the list above. We offer some tips and information about the third possibility in this chapter.

Taking on a trainee

Businesses have a major part to play in the work of training providers. Employer, trainee and training provider are all part of an effective training programme, and so it is important that:

- employers are seen as a partner by the training provider;
- employers see themselves as an equal partner in the arrangement.

A good relationship between employer and training provider is crucial to the success of a training programme, and of course to how successful your trainee is. Your trainee stands a better chance of success if you are involved in:

- designing the training programme;

- making sure that the training provider is given the specifications for the type of person you are looking for;
- making sure that the training provider understands the nature of your business;
- selecting the most suitable candidate for the position;
- training the person to the standards required;
- reviewing the person's progress with the training provider.

How might it work?

1. Initial meeting

Once you have made the decision to take on a trainee, approach a local training provider who will probably arrange a meeting with you to discuss the situation. At this meeting expect the following:

- an outline of the service which the training provider offers;
- an outline of your responsibilities as an employer;
- some initial thoughts about the sort of training which the training provider could arrange to support the trainee while learning at work;
- an explanation of the training provider's health and safety and equal opportunities policies – they are contractually obliged to ensure that you demonstrate good practice in these two areas (they should be able to offer support and advice with this);
- contractual arrangements – your contribution towards the cost of the trainee's allowance will vary; you will be encouraged to take a trainee on as an employee and will receive a grant towards the cost of this; alternatively you may offer a training placement and agree a fee which is paid to the training provider.

2. Selecting a trainee

If you have decided to use the training provider's expertise in selecting a suitable person for your vacancy it is likely that you will be contacted by the training provider with a potential trainee.

Do not expect to have to interview a great number of people yourself. Part of a good training provider's role is to select the most appropriate person for your business, based upon your needs and the people available.

The matching of employer with suitable trainee is a key area of expertise for training providers. Think of it rather like a computer-dating business! If you were looking for a partner you might be lucky enough to find someone who fitted the ideal pattern which you had drawn up in your mind; on the other hand you could waste an awful lot of time meeting people who, as it turned out, were totally unsuitable. It is exactly the same picture when recruiting new staff. A good training provider will want to ensure that the job outline and person specification are clearly written so that they can match the right person for the position.

3. Working with the trainee and training provider
It is likely that your trainee will be taking an NVQ and so becoming familiar with the workings of these qualifications will help you to help him or her. Chapter 6 will give you some background information on NVQs and how to work with your trainee so that he or she achieves competence. The role of the person supervising the trainee is:

- considering what the trainee has to learn;
- planning learning;
- providing opportunities for the trainee to learn;
- coaching and giving feedback;
- assessing the trainee;
- reviewing and evaluating the training.

Building and moving on

Taking on a potential employee for your company is a very important investment. You will be investing a lot of time, money and energy in training and support and so it is a major decision. Once you have made the decision you need to make absolutely sure that you choose the right training provider and the right trainee for your business.

As a result of reading this chapter you are already probably more prepared than many employers to make the most out of your local training provider. As ever, being prepared for the first meeting with the training provider and for the whole process of taking on a trainee will assist both you and the training provider. It will, ultimately, give you a greater chance of recruiting the right person and ensuring that the person receives the best possible support and training.

Getting started

You may have found by asking some of the questions in the 'Taking Stock' section of this chapter that very often people's perceptions of training providers are influenced by hearsay and the experience of others.

It will be important that you feel that you have come to an informed decision about the professionalism of your local training provider. One way to start is by conducting your own survey of local provision. The following suggestions will help.

- Telephone a few of the local training providers. You can often get a feeling of the sort of place it is by the way in which your calls are handled and the response. Do remember though that sometimes training providers give trainees the opportunity to work on reception, so it is worth finding out whether this is the case before coming to any conclusion.
- Going and having a look at a training provider's premises is another good way to check out the type of place it is. Any reputable business should have no qualms at all about showing round prospective clients.
- Talk to trainees currently on the books of the training provider. Ask the manager of the organisation if you can do this. It is a very good quality-check for the organisation, which could obviously learn a great deal from the exercise.
- Talk to employers who are currently involved with youth or adult training. They may have some useful ideas about the way in which the system works, and what the benefits have been to their businesses.

What should you be looking for when carrying out all of the above?

- Well-motivated, business-like, approachable staff who appear to **care** about the welfare of their trainees and the needs of employers.
- A track record of trainees achieving full potential – this may not be just qualifications, or even jobs, but could be examples of

Description of your business
The kind of business this is
Number of employees (full-time/part-time)
My reasons for wanting to take on a trainee
Where the trainee will be working
The type of work the trainee will be expected to do
What I would be looking for in a trainee

Figure 8.1 *Preparation and planning sheet 1*

where trainees have exceeded all expectations or succeeded in difficult circumstances.

- Evidence of employer involvement – do employers come into the training provider? How often are employers visited? What services other than youth and/or adult training does the organisation offer to employers?
- Evidence of trainees' programmes of training – you should ask to see these to check out how off-the-job training will be provided; the units of competence from the NVQ being followed (see Chapter 6) are not really enough as these merely show what the trainee should be achieving, not how s/he is going to achieve them.
- Signs of a partnership approach with employers – the way in which employers are spoken about and described in the promotional literature will tell you whether employers are seen as a necessary evil or gods; a training provider which has an adult

Trainee work activity sheet
Department/area where the trainee will be placed
Person to be directly responsible for the trainee
Summary of duties
Hours of work
Other opportunities for different work experience in the company
Any special conditions or information

Figure 8.2 *Preparation and planning sheet 2*

and business-like relationship with employers is likely to achieve good results.

- Where a training provider is arranging for some of the trainee's training to be carried out at a college, you need to go and have a look at that provision too (see Chapter 7 on using local colleges for more detail on this).
- Where a training provider is delivering some of the trainee's training, the content of the training and its relevance to your business needs to be discussed; again, have a look at a training session in action before making any decision.

Planning each stage in the trainee's progress
It will also help you to make the most of working with a training provider if you have prepared your own systematic approach. You will probably find that the training provider has documentation to

Learning Planner			
Trainee's name			
NVQ being followed			
Unit	Key activities	Where carried out	How carried out

Figure 8.3 *Learning planner*

help both of you plan the training programme for the trainee but it will certainly help if you have given prior thought to each stage of the process as outlined below.

Stage 1: Identify learning opportunities
Before the trainee starts with you, identify broadly the opportunities for learning which exist in your company. Using preparation forms like those shown in Figures 8.1 and 8.2 will ensure that you give the training provider all the information which he or she needs to set up the placement.

Stage 2: Plan the opportunities
Once the trainee has started work within your business you will need to consider the qualification to be sought and how to ensure that the trainee achieves the competences required.

If you have read the other chapters in this book on National Vocational Qualifications (6) and on creating learning opportunities (5) then you are already well prepared for this. It will also help if you sit down with your trainee and look at the NVQ unit-by-unit.

The form shown in Figure 8.3 will help you plan how the activities in each unit will be covered.

Final thoughts

We have looked in this chapter at working with a local training provider to help ensure success for a trainee within your business. Remember:

- Use the opportunity of working with a training provider to learn as much as you can about planning and organising training.
- Your other staff will benefit from the same approach as has been outlined here.
- Having a trainee often inspires many other staff within businesses to think seriously about their own training needs.
- Taking on a trainee becomes just one part of developing the sort of business where everyone is interested in learning new skills, and in keeping records of progress so that qualifications can be achieved.

CHAPTER 9
Choosing and Using an External Consultant

Introduction

This chapter looks at the issue of using a specialist consultant to develop your business by supporting training activities. In Chapter 3, on working one-to-one, you will have already considered the benefits of using someone within the organisation to talk over the issues and problems that you face from day-to-day. This can provide a supportive and informative framework within which to deal with problems and develop your skills further. Sometimes, however, it can be useful to enlist the services of someone who can stand outside the organisation and look at things from a different and objective perspective. This chapter will explore whether this would be a useful way forward for your business and discuss the benefits and implications of such an approach.

Taking stock

To whom do you talk about staff development problems? Sometimes our partners/spouses are willing to listen, but sometimes you may feel that the last thing you want to do is to burden your family with your business problems, especially when it is likely that they may have business problems of their own to contend with. Strangely, talking to complete strangers is sometimes very therapeutic, because they have no pre-conceptions about you or your business. This can sometimes lead people to ask simple, uncluttered questions which get to the heart of a problem very quickly.

What was the issue?	What help did I receive?	What else would have been useful?

Figure 9.1 *Crises points – information and advice*

Expert advice: your experiences

Think back to the major decisions that you have had to face connected with staff development. They might be decisions about:

- developing marketing skills to cope with the need to diversify;
- taking on new staff and training staff to take new responsibilities;
- using new equipment and technology;
- changing management roles and responsibilities.

Who did you choose outside your business to talk over the problems with?
Why did you choose that person?

Now look at what advice you actually received on these occasions.

Figure 9.1 suggests a format for bringing this information together. Use it to make a list of all the crisis points that you have faced, and by the side of it add the information/advice that you received at the time. By the side of that add any other advice or information which would have been useful.

How large is your third column compared to your second? How much additional help can you think of now that would have been useful, even if you did not think of this at the time?

When we need to talk over business decisions or solve thorny problems it is often difficult to find someone who embodies all the qualities of a good listener, is interested and sympathetic to your situation, can be honest and objective in giving you advice, and who also has extensive knowledge of the type of business you operate, indeed the world of business generally.

Of course it is not only business problems that can lead us to seek outside advice. There are many instances in our lives where trying to solve a problem ourselves is not an option.

Think about the times in your life when the skills of a 'specialist' have been called upon. For example, have you ever:

- Been ill and had to see a doctor?
- Faced personal problems and needed to speak to a counsellor?
- Needed a valuation on your property and visited an estate agent?
- Needed to prepare your will and called upon the legal expertise of a solicitor?
- Wanted to develop a new interest or hobby and taken lessons/instructions from an 'expert'?

If any of the above sound familiar, then you have already used a consultant in one form or another, and as we will see in the rest of the chapter, and as is obvious from the above list also, consultants come in all sorts of shapes and sizes!

Like everything, there are advantages and disadvantages to using a consultant.

Consider the people on the above list again, and any other forms of specialist you have used in the past. Make a note of the advantages and disadvantages attached to each one. Use Figure 9.2 to collate the information. The following prompts might be helpful:

- Are they accessible?
- Are they expensive?
- Are they personal or impersonal?
- Do they have time for you?
- Do they communicate clearly or in jargon?

Specialist	Pros of using him or her	Cons of using him or her

Figure 9.2 *Pros and cons of using a specialist*

• How do you know whether they are competent or not?

The pros and cons which you have identified will probably apply equally well to using a training consultant.

Check out your thoughts with a colleague or a business associate. Ask them:

• if they have ever used a consultant;
• if not, why not;
• if they have, what were the benefits;
• what advice they would give you about choosing and using a consultant?

Finding out

Now that we have raised some of the issues about choosing to use a consultant, let's look at some of the background information which will enable you to come to a clearer decision about whether using a training consultant is, or could be, right for you.

Who are consultants?

Consultants are drawn from a wide variety of backgrounds, and can possess a variety of experience, skills and knowledge. Typical backgrounds might be:

- people who have managerial experience in training organisations and/or in managing training departments within large companies and wish to apply these skills to a consultancy role;
- people who are dissatisfied with their current jobs because they do not provide enough challenge or scope for creativity, and who have expertise in the training field;
- people who have retired or been made redundant and who have expertise and wisdom to offer;

Several things will be common to all those who enter consultancy however:

- they have specialist expertise in one or more areas; they offer objective support, advice, information and opinions for a fee;
- they will work as independent contractors, either as self-employed people or as members of a large consortium;
- they will be contracted on a short or long-term basis for a specific fee arrangement, which could be hourly, daily or on a project basis;
- they will work closely with you and your staff, and probably also have access to other associates or consultants as required and agreed.

Why use a consultant?

The most obvious response often is – to provide specialist information or a specialist service to solve a problem which you cannot, or have not the time to, solve yourself. However, if you want to make the most of the consultant's expertise and to plan for the future of your business, it will help if you agree a collaborative way of working with the consultant. This way you, and your staff, are gaining maximum exposure to:

- new ideas about training approaches and about ways of organising your staff development;
- a new way of working, possibly different from your own which can be an example for staff to tap into;
- new ways of looking at problems;
- a new perspective on your business.

Remember:

- new information on your particular training need can also address or throw light on other problems or issues within your business;
- ideas spark off ideas! In other words, the ideas and advice put forward by the consultant will sometimes set you thinking about a whole range of other ideas for new developments within the business;
- an outside specialist looking at an issue can be accepted by staff in a way that you or a colleague may not be; someone deemed to be a specialist will be seen as that by staff – this not only gives the consultant credibility but also shows staff that you are serious about putting in the maximum effort to take the business forward;
- a consultant can help you and your team **learn**; this will help you in the future when dealing with similar issues.

How can a consultant help you?

You might wish to use a consultant to help you deal with a number of staff development issues. For example, in constructing a staff development plan for your business including personal development planning for all your staff, identifying their training needs. Chapter 2 on personal development planning will give you a good basis from which to start, but if you feel that an objective outsider could assist you in introducing this to staff then you might consider using a consultant to help you out.

A consultant could also help with coaching staff and developing managers. Chapter 3 on working one-to-one will help you identify the skills needed to ensure that effective coaching happens within your organisation. Obviously we would hope that eventually your own staff will develop these skills themselves. One way of supporting this process might be to engage the services of a consultant. He or she could act as a coach him/herself, and/or work with prospective coaches observing and giving feedback to support their development.

You might decide to use a training consultant to run in-house training courses for your staff, for a variety of reasons:

- a general need has arisen for staff to develop as a team in order to work more effectively and you feel that an outsider would be the best person to run a meeting to address this issue;

- a specific lack of knowledge has become apparent in, say, health and safety regulations, COSHH regulations or quality systems and you need to employ a consultant to impart this knowledge to your team;
- a specific technical skill development is called for, for example operating a new computer system, and bringing in an outside consultant to run a training session would be most cost-effective and relevant to your business.

Consultancy roles

Consultants might perform several roles while undertaking a piece of work for you. One consultant may favour one approach, another may take a different tack. This will depend on: the way the consultant likes to work; the type of person he or she is; the specifications that **you** feel are appropriate for the work you wish the consultant to do; and/or the contract which you agree with the consultant.

Depending upon the role that you agree the consultant should take, your involvement will vary considerably. Some of the roles which a consultant may take are:

The influencer – a powerful force, who will direct the contract and be very much in charge of the piece of work, perhaps influencing your whole approach to staff development by recommending that you pay it even greater attention in the future.

The information specialist – someone who is an expert in his/her chosen field who may deliver training in that particular specialism.

The fact finder – someone whose main role is to research your staff development needs, by approaches ranging from simply listening to what you have to say, to formal computated questionnaires which would take stock of existing staff skills.

Identifier of alternatives – someone who sets out clearly the alternative solutions to the issue which is being addressed, for example whether or not to recruit a new member of staff or re-train an existing one, and examines the likely consequences of following each alternative.

The objective observer – someone who takes very little part in resolving a particular issue (say introducing an appraisal system) but who helps you, by asking questions and giving you on-going feedback about how you are handling the situation, to reach your own conclusions about what works best for your business.

Of course, many consultants will perform several roles during their time with you. Some roles will demand more involvement from you than others. Remember that a consultant who helps you learn from what he or she is doing, and helps you to feel that you yourself could approach this problem or one like it alone next time, is more valuable in the long term than someone who just comes up with a solution without you.

How do you know whether a consultant is any good?

This is a difficult one. Often people will come recommended to you. References from past clients are obviously a good way of establishing a prospective consultant's track record. Sometimes consultants come to you through other agencies. Some of these agencies, such the DTI, operate an evaluation procedure to check on the work which consultants have done for clients. Of course many consultants will have impressive sounding initials after their names: MBIM (Member of the British Institute of Management), MITD (Member of the Institute of Training and Development), MIPM (Member of the Institute of Personnel Management), but these do not necessarily guarantee a high standard of service. You may wish to ask a consultant to give you some background on what is involved in becoming a member of his or her professional body.

You can also help yourself establish whether a consultant is going to be any good by being prepared for your first meeting. This you can do by detailing the work to be undertaken and considering the skills and qualities you are looking for.

For example, you decide that your business needs help with introducing NVQs for all staff (see Chapter 10 for more detail on this). Having decided that a training consultant is needed to provide the specialist knowledge required, prior to the meeting you could make a list of what you believe is involved in the work:

• technical understanding of our business, and our occupational area particularly;

- knowledge of what is currently available in NVQs to meet our needs;
- contacts/knowledge of potential training providers who could support staff further;
- planning a strategy for getting the NVQ system up and running;
- identifying costs involved.

You then identify the sort of skills and qualities which the consultant should possess:

- ability to listen – we have already done work on the need for staff to gain qualifications and I would want it to be taken into account;
- ability to prioritise and organise the work;
- ability to challenge me – I can be dogmatic!
- some technical background to get to grips with our specific occupational area;
- ability to influence the team to accept the challenges of working towards qualifications;
- technical knowledge of NVQs, including details of workplace assessment and its implications for us.

You then prepare a series of short questions prior to the interview which will also help determine whether the consultant is the most appropriate for this work:

- What work have you done of a similar nature, and with businesses similar to ours?
- Can you show me any examples of reports (with confidential names, addresses and any specific details omitted of course) which you have prepared in the past?
- Can you outline the sort of approach that you take?
- Have you any references from past clients that I could follow up?

and a 'gut feeling' question not for the consultant's ears!

- Could I get on with this person? Do I trust him or her? Do we speak the same language? Does he or she listen?

What can you expect from a consultant?
There will be several phases to any consultant's work.

Phase 1: 'Making contact

An initial meeting where the consultant finds out about your business and establishes what is required;
exploring the background to the issue;
exploring ways in which you could work together.

Phase 2: Agreeing a contract

Identifying what the outcomes of the work should be;
clarifying who should do what;
agreeing the timescale for the work.

Phase 3: Getting to grips with the problem

Identifying the issues/people that will help or hinder progress.

Phase 4: Setting targets

Planning for action within the project.

Phase 5: Putting things into action

Helping people develop the skills to make the most of the results of the work;
tackling the problem;
talking to you about progress and evaluating what is going on;
making any revisions/alterations.

Phase 6: Completion

making sure that you understand sufficiently so that you can carry on where the consultant will leave off;
reviewing the success or otherwise of the project;
presenting you with any paperwork – reports, and, of course, an invoice!

TRAINING FOR THE SMALL BUSINESS

The contract
Make sure that the contract which you sign is clear and specific about what is to be carried out for the fee specified. A contract should include the following:

- The project objectives – these should be SMART: **S**pecific, **M**easurable, **A**greed, **R**ealistic and **T**imerelated.
- The work programme – this should show clearly exactly what the consultant will do, including special materials to be prepared like training plans, etc., and how the consultant will access any resources as necessary (people, files, rooms for meetings, etc.).
- The time-scale of the work and schedule of key events, such as meetings, draft proposals, etc.
- Terms and conditions and fee arrangements.

A clear contract will avoid misunderstandings at any stage of the proceedings.

Building and moving on

Being prepared
Now that we have looked at a mass of information on training consultancy you may be in a better position to think about whether you want to consider it as an option for your business.

Above all, remember that it will help you if you are prepared to use a consultancy project as an opportunity for everyone to learn. The questions in Figures 9.3 and 9.4 will also help.

Ask yourself the following questions:

What has this exercise taught me about the way I implement staff development across the business? What needs to happen now to ensure that everyone has learned fully from the consultant's visit and to ensure that our business has grown in terms of its receptiveness to training and development?

Funding for consultancy work
There are many agencies supplying advice to businesses in the form of consultancy. Some government agencies, for example,

Prepare Yourself

If you have already begun to identify a problem with which a consultant could help, ask yourself:

• What exactly is the issue?

• What role do I want the consultant to play?

• What exactly do I need from the consultant?

Figure 9.3 *Preparing yourself*

Inform and Prepare Staff

Staff will need to know what is happening so that they can take as full a part as necessary and so that they can learn from what is going on.

Talk to them individually or circulate a short questionnaire based on the following:

• What do you think about the issue that the consultant is going to address?
• What would you like to gain from the exercise?
• What would you like the organisation to gain from the exercise?

After the consultancy work has finished ask:

• What have you gained?
• How do you feel the organisation could tackle similar problems in the future?

Figure 9.4 *Preparing staff*

will supply significant funding towards the cost of consultancy. Contact:

The *Department of Trade and Industry* – they operate schemes for businesses to receive consultancy in a number of different areas, pay for up to a half of the costs, and operate an evaluation procedure to ensure that you get what you need from the consultant.

The local *Training and Enterprise Council* – see Chapter 10 for further information.

Local *Enterprise Agencies* – government, local authority and local business funded agencies designed to promote jobs and enterprise, so particularly useful for new businesses.

Rural Development Commission (formally Council for Small Businesses in Rural Areas) – provides advice for small to medium sized businesses in rural areas.

Local training providers – see Chapter 8 for more on this.

Making the most of a consultant

Remember, you are paying for the advice so don't be afraid to assert what you want, and be sure that the consultant knows exactly what that is.

Try to get as many people involved in the consultancy exercise as you can and make sure that you follow up with each individual involved exactly what he or she has learned.

Evaluate the consultancy period carefully. There may be things which worked well for you, others which did not work so well. Keep records of what happened so that you can refer to them next time you come to choose and use a consultant.

CHAPTER 10
Training and Enterprise Councils

Introduction

This chapter looks at the work of Training and Enterprise Councils – TECs – bodies which have a major responsibility for and influence over the training and development of businesses up and down the country. They are only comparatively recently established organisations and so the full impact of their work has not yet been felt. As your business could be a potential user of the services which they provide we will examine their role in this chapter and look at ways in which you could benefit from their work.

Taking stock

What do you know about your local TEC?
When you ask people what they think a TEC is, the same reply comes back again and again: 'The Tech College of course!' Very few people seem to have heard of Training and Enterprise Councils, the organisations launched amid a blaze of publicity in 1989 to foster growth and regenerate local economies.

They have a responsibility in each locality for developing businesses in the area by offering a range of support for training, grants to assist new businesses and coordinating labour market information which businesses can tap into.

As a starting point consider:

What have you heard about TECs, generally or in your locality?
Investigate any places where you feel you might be able to find out more.

You may find it helpful to look in places like the job centres, local libraries, local colleges, community centres, careers offices, chambers of commerce and other local employer networks. Ask the staff in these organisations what they know about the local TEC.

TECs have a responsibility for coordinating information which could be useful to the local business community.

What sort of information would your business find useful? For example, you might have invested in some specialist machinery for a particular contract and need to know about specialist training support, or you might have heard colleagues talking of BS5750 and want to find out more about this.

TECs are locally based to serve the needs of local communities.

What sort of area do you operate within? Is it, for example, rural, inner-city, small town? Are you aware of the population make-up, the population patterns of the different areas within the locality and of the major towns?

What, historically, has been the foundation of the area's economic base? How has this changed in recent years? Are local industries predominantly manufacturing or service-based, for example?

What about the labour force in the area? What have you noticed when recruiting new staff?

Is the local labour force skilled, semi-skilled, unskilled, leading to a skills shortage? What is the proportion of men and women in the labour market? Are there many different ethnic groups within the business community? Are there many older people available for work, having been made redundant or taken early retirement?

All of the above gives a picture of your area.

What are the particular needs of businesses within your locality?

What are your particular needs?

How do these differ from the needs of business on a national basis?

TECs are made up of groups of local business people. We will go on to describe this constitution in more detail in the next section.

> What are your first thoughts on local business people running programmes for local businesses?
>   What might be the advantages and disadvantages of this approach? Make a list and return to it when you have gleaned some more information about TECs, from your own investigations and/or from the next section in this chapter.

Finding out

What are TECs?
Training and Enterprise Councils came into being in England and Wales in 1989. Scotland has made its own, similar, arrangements called Local Enterprise Councils (LECs). A government White Paper in 1988, *Employment in the 1990s*, had highlighted the need for a better trained and more flexible labour force to cope with the rapid pace of change in world markets. In the White Paper, the government invited local groups led by employers to submit proposals for the establishment of bodies (TECs) which would contract with them 'to plan and deliver training and to promote and support the development of small businesses and self-employment within their area'.

This move was a radical shift away from the pattern of training in the past. It proposed:

- giving employers the lead in determining training needs, and thereby hoped to ensure that the training provision would be more relevant to employers' needs and so improve the skills and enterprise of the workforce;
- a coherent approach to training and enterprise at a local level;
- shifting training away from the public sector (the Department of Employment) into private sector organisations, which would need to show through annual accounts how public money was being spent;
- that current government funded training programmes – YTS and ET (see Chapter 8) – could be tailored to meet the needs of business locally, and so introduced flexibility into programmes

155

which had until then been delivered in the same way everywhere in the country.

There are currently 82 TECs in existence in England and Wales and 22 LECs in Scotland. Boundaries are roughly equivalent to county boundaries, although some counties with large cities have more than one TEC (eg, Nottinghamshire has a North Nottinghamshire TEC and a Greater Nottingham TEC), some counties have split up between different TECs (eg, the south of Lincolnshire is covered by the Peterborough TEC) and London has nine TECs in operation.

In short, it was a deliberate move away from:

centralised control over training by the Manpower Services Commission – which was renamed the Training Commission which became the Training Agency and is now the Training, Enterprise and Education Directorate (TEED) of the Department of Employment;

direct government control;

a rather piecemeal approach to training.

It was a deliberate move towards:

local groups serving local needs;

involvement of business leaders, at high levels;

a focused approach of business and education working together to revitalise the local economy through a coordinated approach;

an accent on performance – TECs would be judged on achievement and funded accordingly – so would give better value for money;

an enterprising organisation which would reform training in a bold and far-reaching way.

Who are the people behind TECs?

The government insisted on high-level involvement at board level of TECs. At least two-thirds of TEC boards have to be private sector employers at chairperson or chief executive level. They are there as TEC directors in their own right, and not as representatives of their employer. The remaining members of the board include chief executives or their equivalents from education, economic development, trade unions, voluntary organisations and the public sector.

When they took over from the Training Agency, the newly established TECs needed people on the ground to carry out the various tasks. Staff from the Training Agency local offices were initially seconded to them, ensuring that the new TEC directors had field staff who had experience of training programmes and the local area and labour market.

To a large extent those staff are still working for TECs, although in some cases TECs have employed people from outside to introduce fresh ideas into the organisation. The staff who did move over from being 'civil servants' into being employees of a private company have had a lot of support and training to help them make the shift. A chief executive was appointed to head up this workforce. Often this was the former Training Agency manager, but, again, sometimes a completely fresh face was appointed.

TECs: products, services and responsibilities
Each TEC is in charge of a budget allotted to them by the government. The size of this budget depends on local needs and on the TEC's performance in carrying out its tasks. Overall, TECs have budgets running into millions of pounds of public money, so it is important that they are performance-related to ensure wise spending of this money. It should be noted that currently there is some 'negotiation' underway between key TEC directors and the government because of recent cuts in funding.

Each TEC has shaped its own business plan to reflect and address the economic and social needs of its area. As a starting point, each TEC has the training and enterprise programmes previously run by the Department of Employment, but these are only a start; what is actually on offer can vary from region to region.

The activities and responsibilities which we have outlined below are what **should** and **could** be happening. In the last section of this chapter we will encourage you to be active in finding out if your business community is actually receiving these services, and if not to find out why!

TECs are responsible for:

157

Providing training opportunities for young people. YT is the largest programme here. The TEC is charged with ensuring that the 'Government Guarantee' of a place on a training scheme, with the aim of this leading to vocational qualifications and a job, is met.

Providing opportunities for the unemployed. Employment Training, tailored to the needs of the local community, is the responsibility of the TEC and aims to ensure that unemployed people gain the skills needed for the job market.

Promoting training for the employed. The TEC has designed a variety of training strategies to help local businesses train their workforces. There are some examples of these below.

Business growth. The TEC provides support for both new enterprises and expanding businesses. Business advice in planning, management, marketing and finance is all on offer. More examples of this are listed below.

Education/business partnerships. TECs also fund links between education and business. In Chapter 11 on networks and partnerships we explore the benefits of such an approach.

In most instances the TEC does not provide training and small business assistance directly. It contracts with consultants, training providers and local Enterprise Agencies to deliver the training. It does, however, have a responsibility for ensuring that the subcontractors do their job competently.

Examples of services which TECs offer:

YT and ET, tailored to meet business needs, eg, Employer Partnership scheme which includes training for existing employees and new trainees in one package.

Specialist training for women returners, people with disabilities, ethnic minority groups.

Services to business

New Business Information Seminars for people about to embark on being self-employed, with advice on how to qualify for Enterprise Allowance funding.

Business Planning workbooks to help businesses sort out training and development needs.

Business Enterprise programmes covering business planning.

Business Masterclass seminars to help businesses plan ahead.

Business Growth programmes to develop management skills.

Business Seminars on a range of business topics such as Finance, Marketing, Management.

Training Access Points (TAPs) to provide access through computers to information about local and national opportunities for training and vocational education – these can be found in a variety of places, eg, local libraries, even local supermarkets.

Investors in People. This is a relatively new programme which hopes to ensure that businesses which invest in training for their staff gain recognition for it. A business has to prove that it:

- makes a public commitment from the top to develop all its employees to achieve its business objectives;
- regularly reviews the training and development needs of its employees;
- takes action to train and develop individuals on recruitment and throughout their employment;
- evaluates the investment in training and development to assess achievement and improve future effectiveness.

Businesses working towards the Investors in People award can have support from independent advisors, and are assessed by TEC specialists.

TECs also have an interest in programmes which are still directly managed by TEED regionally. These are:

Technical and Vocational Education Initiative (TVEI) – an initiative in secondary schools and colleges which tries to ensure that the school curriculum is related to the world of work and that young people leave school with skills for working in a technological society.

Work-related Further Education – the post-16 further education provision locally, usually found at the local college.

Other activities in which TECs are involved
The main responsibilities of TECs have been outlined above. There are also other things which TECs across the country are doing which could have an effect on your business, or which your business could make use of. Some of them involve businesses working with other institutions and we have outlined these in more detail in Chapter 11, Networks and Partnerships. Examples of these activities are:

- launching local training awards to recognise investment in training;
- mounting marketing campaigns to secure greater employer commitment to training;
- establishing business clubs in major towns;
- promoting economic development forums;
- involvement in the development of individual action plans for young people in schools so that the idea of personal goal-setting starts early;
- promoting the use of open learning within firms;
- promoting training exchanges with overseas companies;
- sponsoring mobile training facilities for people who find it difficult to travel;
- promoting support for minority groups, particularly ethnic community-based training and cooperative businesses, training for disabled people and establishing nursery/crèche facilities to help women returning to paid employment;
- sponsoring teacher placements within industry and joint management courses for head teachers and business executives;
- developing tele-working to help people in rural areas.

Building and moving on

Making the most of the local TEC
So how can you make the most of your local TEC? How can you ensure that you obtain what you need, both as an individual and as a business?

Below are a few ideas. The thing to remember is that a local TEC is there to serve local needs, and it will help if they are kept informed as to what those local needs are by the people who matter: local businesses and potential users of the services which they provide.

The following checklist provides a starting point:

Checklist for Making the Most of Your TEC

- Form networks and make use of existing ones – see Chapter 11, Networks and Partnerships, for more ideas on this. By collaborating in requesting services from the TEC you stand more chance of getting what you need.
- Get together a business plan and an outline of your key objectives as a business. You will have already started to do this in the opening chapter of this book – Making the Most of Your Business. Then ask for a meeting at the TEC to discuss this and find out how the TEC can help you in achieving your objectives.
- Keep a look out for one-off seminars/conferences/events which the TEC might be sponsoring – sometimes these are free.
- Make enquiries about the way the TEC operates. Some of them have Regional Boards/Advisory Committees in place. It may be that you could learn and make good contacts through being part of these.
- Make sure your voice is heard – TECs are not responsible themselves for delivering training but need to know what you need to inform training providers.
- Find out how the TEC ensures the quality of its training provision, from YT and ET providers to business training. This links to the next point.
- Take action if you see poor quality training provision. In Chapters 8, 7 and 9 on using training providers, colleges and consultants, we have given some ideas on how to come to informed decisions about whether you are getting value for money in using these organisations/individuals. If you come across examples of TEC-funded training not being organised correctly then don't sit on the fence. Bring your complaint to the organisation and if you get no satisfaction take it to the TEC.
- Investigate the Investors in People award. If you have made a start on training and developing your people by reading this book, and put into practice all of the suggestions that are in

---

here, it is likely that you are already well on the way to being an Investor in People. Why not gain some public recognition for it?

- Talk about TEC services with others. The more people know about them, the more influence businesses have.

CHAPTER 11
Networks and Partnerships

Introduction

Competition is everywhere. It has always been a watch-word in commercial organisations but it has becoming increasingly important in education, health care, and in public transport, to name but a few areas. Healthy competition can, of course, be very beneficial: it can keep businesses sharp, responsive and innovative. If they do not provide the needed product or service in the right way, at the right time and at the right price, then someone else will step in!

Competition can, however, be unhealthy and destructive. If individuals and businesses channel energies into their own success at the expense of others, then this success is likely to be short-lived. A strong, healthy economy is the only way to secure long-term success rather than the dangerous short-term gain. Indeed there are times when working with others is the only way of achieving maximum gain! Cooperating, complementing and collaborating become key words as well as competing!

The focus on re-cycling in recent years offers an example. A business may set up in an area, having seen the commercial potential in re-cycling a range of materials. The business will benefit enormously if there are partners willing to cooperate in the collection of suitable materials. For example:

supermarkets, garages and schools might offer to be collection points;
parish/district councils might enhance the collection facilities further;
local media will be involved in publicity;
voluntary organisations might wish to get involved – providing

a door-to-door collection service, and raising funds in the process; schools and colleges could provide further support by working with the business in a collaborative educational project and informing and educating people to change habits and 'think green';
a local business network might contribute to any of the above and demonstrate the commitment of its members to an important local initiative by changing its use or re-use of materials.

Everyone involved in such a project would stand to gain in one way or another, yet the commercial viability would not be lessened for the re-cycling company. The key words here would be **networks and partnerships**: people, businesses and other groups working together for the benefit of everyone.

This approach is important and relevant in many ways to education and training. To make the most of the learning opportunities, resources and facilities around, there needs to be:

• cooperation and collaboration to ensure training needs are met – fully covered – but without unnecessary duplication. Choice – yes; confusion – no!
• effective partnerships to ensure both the theoretical and practical aspects of any training programme are covered: certain things are best learned initially away from the pressure of work; others need to be acquired in the real work situation;
• effective ways of sharing information, ideas and good practices.

Taking stock

Your business connections
Before we look at ways in which networks and partnerships can be developed to support effective training and learning, it is worth exploring what is around already. As with all things, more harm than good can be done by enthusiastically setting up a new group with plans to 'sort things out'. This approach frequently fails through lack of consistent, long-term support, resentment from those who have already been trying their best and a lack of

understanding of past history and experiences. So start by thinking about your business networks:

What connections does your business have with other businesses, organisations, groups, associations, etc., both private and public sector?
What about you as an individual?
What about others in your business?

As well as considering what networks you and others have, think about their value:

How do you currently use your connections? What is helpful and useful to your business and what is not?
How could you make more of them? What changes, developments and improvements would you like to see and why?

This will give you an overview of the current situation with networks and partnerships in **your business**.

Local support: what is available?

How about other networks and partnerships? It would be worth carrying out some research to find out what is around and available locally to support and help with training and development for small/medium sized organisations. (This could be a useful project for someone – see Chapter 5, Creating Learning Opportunities.) Here is a list of useful starting points for your research:

The local TEC – Training and Enterprise Council (and see Chapter 10).
TEED – the Training, Enterprise and Education Directorate of the Employment Department at Moorfoot, Sheffield, for details of TECs and other initiatives in your area.
Local education institutions: colleges, schools, polytechnics, universities – ask for the industry liaison or business development officer/manager.
Libraries.
Chamber of Commerce.
Professional associations relating to your type of business.

Local MCI network – the Management Charter Initiative is working to set up a national network to encourage professionalism, training and education in management.

Local branches of:

ITD – Institute of Training and Development
IPM – Institute of Personnel Management
WIT – Women in Training
WIM – Women in Management.

Business supplements in local newspapers and magazines.
Trade journals/directories.
Rural Development Commission.
Economic Development Unit or Inner City Development Unit.
Local Careers Office.
Employer networks and associations.
Small Business Clubs.
Industry training organisations.
Job Centre.

This should give you a good picture of how local organisations are working – or not working – together in partnerships and networks to support and develop good education and training locally. Keep a list/database of organisations, contact names and current activities.

Finding out

Examples of good practice
There are around the country many good examples of partnerships and networks working effectively. The following is a list of ideas and activities which you may wish to explore further. You are not likely to find all of these operating in your area, but you will probably find some!

An education-business partnership – probably set up and supported by the local TEC to coordinate and develop all education-business links and activity.

A compact – likely to be an inner-city initiative: a 'deal' in which employers undertake to provide jobs with training if young people meet certain goals (completion of courses, obtaining certain qualifications, maintaining agreed standards of time-keeping and attendance, etc.).

TVEI – The Technical and Vocational Education Initiative – set up to enrich the curriculum for young people aged 14–18 by linking education clearly to the working world, developing work experience and involving people from industry and commerce in curriculum planning and development.

DTI – Department of Trade and Industry Enterprise and Education Initiative – set up to promote work experience, teacher secondments and industry-based teacher-training.

Sponsorship schemes – in which local businesses may sponsor certain courses, students or education and training initiatives; could include cash, equipment, resources, etc. Many businesses agree to offer local schools and colleges surplus materials for practical and project work or to loan equipment or offer the use of their premises.

Governors – the government is currently encouraging business men and women to be involved actively in local schools and colleges as governors to contribute their business expertise and to work with educational staff for effective development of all aspects of these organisations.

Teacher placements, exchanges, shadowing schemes, visiting speakers – there have been a number of interesting examples:

teachers working in local companies as part of their training and development;
teachers applying their skills to the business context, eg, language teaching, computer software applications as well as more general 'people' skills such as training business people in mentoring, tutoring and counselling skills;
teachers and lecturers acting as specialist consultants, using, for example, college resources and equipment to solve technical problems and carry out product trials;
business managers and head teachers shadowing each other to share ideas and expertise and learn from different approaches

as well as understanding better the needs of and pressures on their respective organisations;

business people acting as guest speakers, lecturers or project leaders for a range of educational projects in colleges and schools; in particular offering expertise and support to young enterprise/student 'mini-businesses';

local employers offering to run 'mock' recruitment/selection/ interview sessions for school and college leavers;

local business involvement in careers conventions, careers training and information.

Work experience and training placements – businesses not only offer the placement for work experience but actively get involved in designing and delivering the training, working with colleges, schools and training providers.

Business problems – local colleges and institutions of higher education ask local businesses to act as case studies and submit real business projects and problems of all kinds for students to work on under expert guidance.

Professional training and development courses – with the new NVQ system and a new range of competence-based management qualifications, there are currently useful trials with managers from education, industry and commerce attending the same training courses, forming useful networks, sharing experiences and problems.

Business clubs and clusters – sometimes organised formally by a college or other organisation, the purpose might be:

to act as a 'learning set': sharing problems, offering advice and expertise;

to pool resources and equipment to save individual expenditure;

to give strength when negotiating with colleges, TECs and other external providers. In some rural areas 'telecottages' have been established, providing a central resource of equipment and technology for individuals and small businesses to use;

to offer workspace to similar/associated businesses for the benefit of all, eg, the local health centre in a restored warehouse where there is a chemist, a homeopathic practitioner, an osteopath, stress counsellors, a fitness studio and health food stores;

to organise their own training cost-effectively, sharing the costs of buying in consultants, training materials (videos, learning materials, etc.), guest speakers, etc.

European links – educational establishments often arrange student exchanges in Europe and even further afield and businesses of course export. Often links can be shared and enhanced with a partnership approach – work placements for students abroad, business and education joint visits, exchanges, etc.

These should have given you some ideas about the kinds of activities currently taking place; no doubt you will uncover more in your local area and you and your colleagues will have new ideas for networks and partnerships.

Benefits of effective networking

Reading through the list above will give you some idea of how your business could benefit through getting involved in some networking; it will probably also have suggested ways in which **you** could contribute. It is worth remembering the benefits, particularly when you are trying to encourage the support of others:

- the opportunity for local business people to be involved actively in the development and implementation of the educational curriculum;
- education and business having a better understanding of each other's needs and problems;
- contributing to the development of a motivated, educated, trained and enterprising workforce – crucial to business success;
- learning new skills, gaining access to a range of expertise and experience in a number of very cost-effective ways;
- gaining appropriate support – avoiding the isolation which can often be a problem for managers of small businesses;
- having a strong voice – it is too easy for the needs and opinions of the small business to be overlooked by large organisations and in national initiatives;
- creating a very wide range of learning opportunities – far more than could be possible within one business and thus keeping new ideas and approaches regularly coming in.

Using a collaborative approach successfully

As with any successful group or team, there are a number of key factors which contribute to effectiveness and achievements. The following checklist will not only help you set up useful groups but also give you some ideas for influencing any in which you might become involved.

Checklist for successful collaboration

- Discuss and agree the purpose with all those involved.
- Be committed to building on existing success and to improving and developing new things.
- Set Specific, Measurable, Agreed, Realistic, Time-related objectives – but these might well be quite few and simple!
- Monitor, evaluate and review activity and achievement to find what has worked well and what has not; learn from this and act accordingly.
- Agree a way of working with which everyone involved feels comfortable – this could be written as a simple code of practice – to avoid any misunderstandings.
- Allow time for people to get to know and understand each other before tackling anything too ambitious; be aware of people's different concerns, starting points and personal 'agendas'.
- Recognise and publicise successful activities.

Building and moving on

Considering the possibilities

You have now had the opportunity to think about your current involvement with a number of external groups and organisations. You have also been given some information about the kinds of networks and partnerships where businesses and other organisations have successfully carried out a number of activities. You now need to think about the following when considering possible networks and partnerships:

- what you could do;

- what you – and others in your business – want to do;
- what you most need;
- what you have to offer.

Your decisions should be helped by many of the preceding chapters in this book. For example, sorting out your business objectives and personal development plans will give you a very good idea of what your priorities are for the business as a whole and for making the most of your people. You will be able to consider possible business networks or links with education as being appropriate in helping you achieve these objectives and plans.

In many ways, it will be something of a matching process: looking at your wants and needs and what the various groups are offering; conversely, looking at the needs and wants of the groups and considering what you have to offer.

You may be in an area where there is much enthusiasm for networking and partnerships and where your interest, enquiries or offers are welcomed and encouraged. You may find that you have the opportunity to make your needs known and influence what local groups do. Lucky you! You stand to gain much, as do the people in your business.

However, you are likely to find things to be more patchy. There may be a number of groups but they may not be very active or innovative: the small business club which has become a rather purposeless talking or moaning shop, for example. You may decide to join, or to continue to try to work with one or two like-minded people to change things gradually from within. You might be able to use some of the ideas, checklists and information in this book to help you!

Starting your own network

You may decide to start a network of your own. One small group of business managers we know meets regularly and informally every fortnight. Each meeting is devoted to one particular business: any problem can be aired, idea explored, difficult situation discussed. Success is far more likely when several people with a range of backgrounds and experiences, yet with similar daily responsibilities and roles, all apply their brain-power. It is a very effective 'learning set'. It would be relatively easy for this small, informal group to extend its activity – should its members so wish.

- They could invite new members from different businesses to join them to extend the scope and range of their experience and expertise.
- They could invite – and if necessary share the costs of – a guest speaker or consultant.
- They could negotiate with a local college or training provider to run a particular course on to which each could send two representatives – if, for example, they all wish for training in export legislation.
- They could support each other through a particularly challenging project, for example working for accreditation to BS5750 – the quality systems standard.
- They could between them offer an excellent training programme to a local youth training provider whereas one on his/her own might only be able to offer a limited range of experience.
- They could invite a representative from the local TEC to come and discuss current support and training for small businesses and, at the same time, present their needs and wants to the TEC.

The possibilities are limited only by your creativity and commitment! We firmly believe that working with others – in a variety of networks and partnerships – is an excellent way of developing a very wide range of learning and training opportunities.

So, consider some alternatives; make some decisions; set some objectives; devise a plan of action and get going!

Summary

Learning is a key word in this book. We hope that you will learn:

directly from some of the ideas and suggestions in the book;
more indirectly by discussing and sharing these ideas and
exchanging experiences with other people;
by your own experience of applying these ideas in your
business;
by examining your successes and less successful attempts to
introduce new ideas; of course much can be learned from
studying what went wrong but we sometimes forget to analyse
the reasons why something worked well!

Above all, we would hope that the sum total of all that learning
will add up to a thriving business where everyone is encouraged to
learn, question and re-think.

We realise that there is a lot to be done to achieve this position.
There are several ways in which you could make a start; below we
list some suggestions:

- Go back to the 'Your Business' section in Chapter 1, Making the
  Most of Your Business. Look again at the activities which we
  suggested you carry out to take stock of your current business
  position. These will provide you with the basis for setting
  objectives for your business and identifying broad training
  needs.
- Introduce the ideas in this book to your staff. This could be done
  individually, or, if numbers permit, as a group. Above all, this
  would be an opportunity to show your commitment to learning
  and to gain the team's support for continual training and
  development.

- Construct some simple personal development plans for each member of your staff which outline clearly his or her agreed objectives and the ways by which these will be met. You will need to refer back to the ideas in other chapters of the book to ensure that you have considered every learning opportunity available to your staff, both inside and outside the business.
- Collaborate with a colleague from another business (see Chapter 11, Networks and Partnerships) to plan a way forward. This could be followed up with regular meetings to share problems and discuss progress.
- If you feel inspired by the ideas in the book but daunted by the magnitude of the task ahead you could

  - use an outside consultant to set the ball rolling;
  - re-think roles and responsibilities within the existing staff structure and create a new role, that of staff development manager;
  - collaborate with a colleague from another business (see above) to plan a joint strategy which includes co-funding and co-recruiting an external consultant or a part-time/full-time staff development manager.

We are sure you will think of many more possibilities. Above all, remember that you do not need to rush in and implement all of the ideas in the book at once. Start gradually, but set clear and achievable objectives so that you can monitor progress and build upon what works best for your business. As one eminent business consultant put it:

'JUST DO IT!'

Make a start somewhere. Good luck.

Appendix

Useful addresses

Department of Trade and
  Industry
Kingsgate House
66–74 Victoria Street˜
London SW1E 6SW

Telephone: 071-215 2574

Institute of Personnel
  Management
IPM House
35 Camp Road
Wimbledon
London SW19 4UW

Telephone: 081-946 9100

Institute of Training and
  Development
Marlow House
Institute Road
Marlow
Bucks SL7 1BD

Telephone: 0628 890123

MCI (Management Charter
  Initiative)
Russell Square House
10–12 Russell Square
London WC1B 5BZ

Telephone: 071-872 9000

National Council for Vocational
  Qualifications
222 Euston Road
London NW1 2BZ

Telephone: 071-387 9898

Rural Development Commission
141 Castle Street
Salisbury Wilts SP1 3TP

Telephone: 0722 336255

Scottish Development Agency
Small Business Division
Rosebery House
Haymarket Terrace
Edinburgh EH12 5EZ

Telephone: 031-337 9595

Scottish Vocational Education
  Council
Hanover House
24 Douglas Street
Glasgow G2 7NQ

Telephone: 041-248 7900

Training Enterprise and Education
  Directorate
Employment Department
TEC Development Unit
Moorfoot Sheffield S1 4PQ

Telephone: 0742 753275

Welsh Development Agency
Business Development Unit
Business Development Centre
Treforest Industrial Estate
Pontypridd
Mid Glamorgan CF37 5UT

Telephone: 0443 841777

Women in Management
64 Marryat Road
Wimbledon
London SW19 5BN

Telephone: 081-944 6332

Examination boards

Business and Technology
   Education Council
(BTEC)
Tavistock House South
Tavistock Square
London WC1A 9LG

Telephone: 071-413 8500

City and Guilds of London
   Institute
(CGLI)
46 Britannia Street
London WC1X 9RG

Telephone: 071-278 2468

Pitmans Examinations Institute
Catteshall Manor
Godalming
Surrey GU7 1UU
Telephone: 0483 415311

RSA Examinations Board
Westwood Way
Coventry CV4 8HS

Telephone: 0203 470033

Further reading

We have found the following books enjoyable and practical.

Handy, C (1990) *Inside Organisations*, BBC Publications.
This is written in an 'easy-to-read' style and is deliberately friendly, undogmatic and accessible. The ideas contained within, however, are challenging, far-reaching, exciting and humane.

Harvey-Jones, J (1988) *Making It Happen*, Fontana/Collins.
A spendid anecdotal read based on the writer's rich and varied experience which contains much common-sense advice on all aspects of business life and management.

Clemmer, J and McNeil, A (1989) *Leadership Skills for Every Manager*, Piatkus.
This book presents a complete and detailed picture of the contexts in which managers need to operate today, together with the skills and qualities they need.

Blanchard, K and Johnson, S (1982) *The One Minute Manager*, Fontana/ Collins.
A very short, easy-to-read book. Some people consider the ideas rather simplistic; others find them uncluttered and practical.

Allan, J (1989) *How to Solve your People Problems*, Kogan Page.
A practical guide which deals with topics such as delegation, motivation, difficult people, negotiation, conflict, discipline, appraisal, recruitment and so on.

Honey, P (1980) *Solving People Problems*, McGraw-Hill.
A focused, practical book for managers with lots of case studies and examples of how to work to encourage the behaviour you want and discourage inappropriate behaviour.

Garratt, B (ed) (1985 on) The Successful Manager Series, Fontana.
A comprehensive series of short paperbacks dealing with a range of management topics such as managing change, developing teams, time management, recruitment and selection, career management.

Nicholson, J (1992) *How do you Manage?* BBC Books.
Accompanies the recent BBC series of the same name. A straightforward book covering many aspects of managing self and people.

Buckley, R and Caple, J (1991) *One-to-One Training and Coaching Skills*, Kogan Page.
This book offers clear and practical advice on how to design and implement training seminars tailored to individual needs for delivery in a one-to-one or 'Sitting by Nellie' training approach.

Fletcher, S (1991) *NVQs, Standards and Competence*, Kogan Page.
Provides a comprehensive overview of the key concepts and issues underpinning the competence/NVQ movement and offers guidance on the preparation, implementation and maintenance of a competence-based standards programme.

Fletcher, S (1992) *Competence-Based Assessment Techniques*, Kogan Page.
An explanation of competence-based assessment, its purposes and uses is offered in this book, together with guidelines on how to implement such a system.

Index